Contents

1 Practice Planning 1

2 Interval Training Conditioning 9

3 Skating Drills 17

4 Puck Control Drills 37

5 Passing and Shooting Drills 43

6 Individual Drills 107

7 Team Drills 137

Introduction

This book is designed for ready and continual use by coaches. Flipping through the pages will give the coach his desired drills. The coach should use the drills that will serve his purpose and his strategy. Do not use a drill that runs counter to your strategy or philosophy of the game. Pick the drills that will give your team maximum benefit and be willing to make variations or alterations to a drill to make it better fit your needs.

Plan your practices to move quickly and efficiently. Do not let dead time creep into your practices. Move from one drill to the next drill in an organized manner. Drills that have the players handing on the boards waiting too long for their turns creates a listless practice. The players' conditioning is enhanced with the players in constant motion.

Make your drills as close as possible to game conditions. Put time limits on the drills. Use pressure tactics like so many passes before the shot on goal. A drill is performed in practice in game-like conditions so that when it does occur in a game situation, the players will know how to react. Drills that have no game situation basis may be of little value as the skill transfer to game conditions has little meaning to the player.

Always keep "fun" in your practices and planning. We are not advocating a slapstick approach to coaching. Remember that the game should be fun, not just for the players but also for the coaches. Enjoy the process.

There is one basic rule to practice planning and that is, **"If it can happen during a game, it must be practiced."** Never assume that something is such a simple procedure that there should be no problems during game conditions. Game conditions are pressure situations and the simple requirements do not always work under pressure.

SPALDING®

HOCKEY

skills

Dr. Gerald A. Walford

& Gerald E. Walford

MASTERS PRESS

SPORTS PUBLISHER

A Division of Howard W. Sams & Co.

Masters Press (A Division of Howard W. Sams & Co.)
2647 Waterfront Pkwy. E. Drive, Suite 300
Indianapolis, IN 46214

Library of Congress Cataloging-in-Publication Data
Walford, Gerald A.,

      Spalding hockey skills / Gerald A. Walford and Gerald E. Walford.
         p.   cm. -- (Spalding sports library)
    ISBN 0-940279-78-9
    1. Hockey -- Training.   I. Walford, Gerald E.,
  II. Title. III. Title: Hockey skills. IV. Series.
  GV848.3.W35   1993   93-45337
  796,962'07 -- dc20   CIP

Credits:
  Cover design by Julie Biddle
  Cover photo by Frank S. Howard
  Diagrams by Julie Biddle
  Type Design by Leah Marckel

1
Practice Planning

Coaching is a year-round job, even at the youth program level. The off-season should be used to formulate plans and organize for the coming season. Beginning the season in an orderly manner will enhance a smooth progression from the off-season to the preseason to the season. Good organization will give the players a feeling of confidence with the coach and management. Disruptions will occur, but the well-prepared coach will be ready to meet these disruptions. A coach when planning should always plan for "Murphy's Law": whatever can go wrong, will go wrong. A coach that plans for problems will be prepared when and if they occur. This type of coach is a well-prepared coach.

PRESEASON ARRANGEMENTS

Arrangements for facilities, equipment, and training should be made before the season starts. Many of these things will be done during the off-season. If they are done during the off-season, they should be checked and verified during the preseason so that all systems are go for the season.

GOALS AND OBJECTIVES

In practice planning, the coach must determine his short range and long range goals or objectives. Just what does he want to accomplish? Do these objectives fit into the coaches philosophy? A coach needs objectives and philosophy to determine the direction of the team. No direction—no plan—no accomplishment. A lack of these qualities leads to disorganization and even chaos. Once the objectives and philosophies are set, plan to meet these criteria. Practice planning is a combination of long range goals and short term goals. The coach must develop his long range goals from his philosophy of the game. His desired style of play for the season or

1

future years are part of the long range goal. His short term goals are a lead-up to his long range plans and his philosophy. Planning takes time and should not be treated lightly. Plan so that you know where you are going and how you are going to get there.

DRESSING ROOM TALKS

To save ice time, the coach should do his talking and explaining in the dressing room before going on the ice. A chalk board or any other type of visual aid can be used to explain the practice and drills to the players. This means ice time is saved by not having to explain things on the ice. Long discussions on the ice is dead time. Sometimes on-ice discussions are needed, but, if ice time is expensive and you are only allowed so much time on your budget, keep the on-ice practice moving and save the long talks for the dressing room.

DEMONSTRATION

In most cases, the coach should have his players demonstrate. This gives recognition to the players and helps with the confidence of the team. With the players demonstrating, the coach is free to comment on technique and point out the key points in the skill. As a coach gets older, his demonstrations may not be as good as he thinks they are. Some coach's demonstrations may seem to be a means of "showing off" or showing how good he is. Be careful, do not let this happen to you. Some coaches demonstrate because they do not know how to adequately comment on the technique. They know how to do the skill, but they do not know how to teach the skill. Another important consideration in demonstrations is that when one demonstrates, the observers or players will focus on the results of the demonstration and not on the technique of the skill. For example, if the coach is demonstrating the slap shot, the players will focus on how accurate or powerful his shot is and not on his technique. To help the players focus on the technique, the coach must tell the players what to look for. Slow motion demonstrations can help focus on a certain part of the skill. Also, demonstrations of just going through the motion without shooting the puck can be helpful.

EVALUATION

It is a good idea for the coach to keep his practice plans for rechecking and evaluation. If a coach finds that his breakout play is not working, he can check his plans for time allotment on the breakout play. If the check reveals that insufficient time was spent on the breakout, future practices can be adjusted accordingly. If sufficient time was given to the breakout play, the coach must decide as to why it is not working. Perhaps the learning situation was not good, maybe the coaching was inadequate, maybe the style of teaching is not working with this group, or maybe the players are slow learners. These are difficult questions to answer honestly. It is not easy to say the coaching was weak despite all the work and effort that went into the practices. Work and effort at times are not enough; it is the result that counts. Evaluate honestly and correct your errors.

FLEXIBILITY AND CHANGE

The practice plans should remain flexible for changes. If some phases are not progressing as fast as predicted then future sessions have to be adjusted to meet this demand. The plan for the day; however, should usually remain the same. Adjustments are for the next day. Too many last minute adjustment during the day plan will throw off the overall schedule. If 15 minutes is allowed for penalty killing and success is not achieved in this time, move on to the next drill and adjust the plan for tomorrow and other succeeding practice sessions. By doing this procedure, the coach will not fail to practice an important phase of the game and will have time after the practice to better analyze the situation for corrective measures.

DRILLS

It must be remembered that drills are only a supplement to the team's strategy or style of play. Indiscriminate use of drills may not achieve the goals or objectives of the team. Do not use a drill just because you think it looks good. The drills must fit into the teams offensive and defensive patterns of play. Be selective. The drills in this book are a sample of possibilities. Good coaches will change and alter some of the drills to fit their needs. New drills should be added to this collection as the season develops. The key to good drill design is to make the drills as close to game situations as possible. As the season progresses, the coach should be able to design drills that will help with the team weaknesses. This book will work well with the book *Coaching Hockey* by the same authors. Many of the drills are designed for the various formations of hockey strategy. Each drill is named for identity. Through repetition of the drills the players will soon learn where to line up and how to execute a drill when it is announced by the coach. The names of the drills are almost a brief description of the drill so it is very easy for the players to learn the drills by name.

A drill is a drill, is a drill,... Never assume that because you do a drill, the players will execute the skill practiced under game conditions. Some coaches practice drills so well that the players are excellent at the drill but fail or are below expectations when the drill situation occurs during a game. Youngsters are particularly vulnerable to this occurrence. Do a drill and then show how it is part of the overall game plan. Then practice the drill under game conditions so that the players are aware of how the skill practiced applies to game conditions. In most cases, the coach will have to go back to the drill again and repeat the game condition practice again. This repeating of the drill, game condition of the drill, drill again, and back to game condition situation must be practiced many times. Remember — coordinate the drill with the game condition scrimmage. Never assume that learning from the drill will transfer to game situations. It is the job of the coach to make learning transfer from drill to game.

Many youth program coaches have little time to prepare for practices. This book can help in that the coach can take a quick look through the book before practice to organize his plan for the day. This is not an ideal situation, but youth coaches do not always have enough time to plan, and so they must do as best they can.

The drills are divided into several skill sections such as skating, passing, shooting, individual and team play. Rarely does a section involve only one skill. Shooting drills usually combine skating, passing, shooting, and some strategy, so use and devise drills that cover as many skills as possible in the same drill.

Practices need variety, interest, and spirit. This is usually no problem in the early season. It is the midseason and late season where this becomes a major concern. Through repetition, the drills become boring and routine. The players may end up going through the motions. To keep up interest and help eliminate the devastating side effects of loss of interest, try not to overwork a drill. If a drill becomes boring, add variations or changes or even drop the drill for awhile. Do not use only one drill to accomplish an objective, use a variety of drills. Keep the practices interesting and fun. Have some humor in your practices. Make it a joy for the players to come to practice.

PRACTICE PLANNING

The coach should outline what he wants to develop for the season. This season plan is then broken down into smaller units, perhaps weekly or two week units. The units are then broken down into the individual practice session. The following is a sample plan.

SAMPLE PRACTICE PLAN

Weekly time schedule

Monday	90 minutes
Tuesday	90 minutes
Wednesday	0 minutes
Thursday	60 minutes
Friday	60 minutes
Saturday	game
Sunday	0 minutes
Total	300 minutes

Weekly Breakdown

Skating and conditioning	60 minutes
Puck control	30 minutes
Offense	30 minutes
Defense	30 minutes
Game situations	120 minutes
Miscellaneous	30 minutes
Total	300 minutes

Daily plan

6:00 to 6:10 — Warm up
  • Laps — 2 minutes
  • Figure 8 — 2 minutes
  • Skate the square — 2 minutes
  • Stops and starts — 2 minutes
  • Lateral mobility — 2 minutes
6:10 to 6:20 — passing and shooting
  • Double give and go — 3 minutes
  • Obstacle passing — 3 minutes
  • Four corner both ways passing drill — 6 minutes
6:20 to 6:30 — individual play
  • Defensemen — sponge puck block drill
  • Forwards — behind the net forechecking
6:30 to 6:40
  • Three on zero both ways — 3 minutes
  • Three on two both ways — 7 minutes
6:40 to 6:50 — attack from breakout
  • 5 on 2 breakout
6:50 to 7:00 — conditioning
  • 3 man races
  • stop and starts on lines
  • backward skating to side boards
  • laps
  • tandem push, pull and wrestle

MASTER PRACTICE SHEET

This sheet is an easy way to keep a record of the practices.

All the skills or practice situations are listed in a column. The time spent (in minutes) on each phase is simply filled in under the date column.

Sample Master Sheet

November	1	2	3	4	5
Conditioning	10	20	10		
Skating	10				
Stickhandling		5			
Passing		5	10		
Shooting		5	10		
Checking					
Goaltending	10	20			
Defensemen	10				
Forwards	10				
Offensive Play		20			
Defensive Play	10				
Face-offs	10				
Penalty Killing	20				
Power Play			20		
Pulled Goalie					
Line Change			10		
Delayed Penalty					
Broken Stick					
Injuries					
Scrimmage			15		

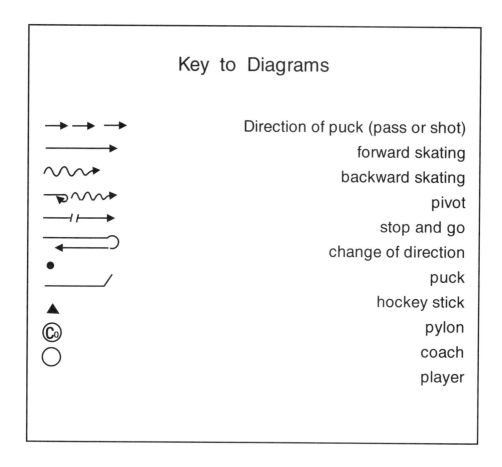

Key to Diagrams

Direction of puck (pass or shot)

forward skating

backward skating

pivot

stop and go

change of direction

puck

hockey stick

pylon

coach

player

2
Interval Training Conditioning

Interval training is a systematic conditioning program by which the subject alternates periods of work with periods of rest. It is these alternating intervals which give the training it's name.

Track and swimming coaches have developed and used this type of training most effectively. Many feel that the interval training program is the cause of the increased rash of record breaking performances. This chapter is an adaptation of this successful interval program to ice hockey.

Interval training is a specificity program. This means that an individual trains to his particular sport of skill. For example, the 220 yard dash man will train differently than the 880 yard runner. To specifically adapt this program to hockey, it had to be determined exactly what a hockey player did when performing and what was happening to his body while performing. To answer this, forwards, defensemen, and goaltenders were charted as to distance and type of skating. The types of skating recorded were forward, backward, and quick breaks.

Blood, speed, respiratory and heart tests were also taken. The blood tests were to evaluate the energy requirements of aerobic and anaerobic systems. With this knowledge and interval training program was developed to closely resemble the body stress of game conditions.

DEFINITION OF TERMS

To understand the explanation of the program, the following terms must be understood.

Training—the exercise program to develop energy potential (conditioning) as well as skill of performance. Training should be applied to the work intervals of this program to enhance the skill level.

Conditioning — a program to develop energy potential only; not concerned with skill development and performance.

Work Interval — the phase of the program in which the athlete is working or performing.

Relief or Rest Interval—the time between work intervals and also the time between sets (resting or recovery phase).

Repetitions—the repeating of work and rest intervals.

Sets — a series of work and rest intervals (a series of repetitions).

The training program is accomplished by manipulating the following factors:

1. Time and distance of work interval.
2. Number of repetitions and sets.
3. Rest or relief interval (time between work intervals).
4. Type of activity during relief interval (e.g. complete rest or light skating).
5. Number of workouts per week.

The coach will have to manipulate these factors to suit his team's age, skill, condition, and number of practice sessions.

For example the coach can have the players skate back and forth between the side boards for forty seconds with an eighty second rest. Such a work/relief interval is called a 1:2 ratio (since the rest is twice as long as the work interval). If the relief interval is increased to 120 seconds with the same 40 second work interval, the ratio would become 1:3. A 1:1 ratio would be a 40 second work interval with a 40 second relief interval.

The relief or rest interval should be sufficient to let the player's heart rate return to 140 beats per minute or less between repetitions. Neglecting this principle of the heart beat will retard development. In individual sports like swimming and track, the athlete can easily count his own heart beat and proceed with his workout. However, in a team sport where the coach wants his players working together, he must regulate his ratio so that before the work interval the entire team has had sufficient time for their heart rates to drop below the 140 beats per minute rate.

The number of repetitions will also vary. For example, repeat three times the back and forth drill between the side boards to a 40 second work interval and an 80 second rest. For example, 0:40 - 1:20 x 3 (notice that the work interval is always first).

Once this repetition is done three times it is called a set. More than one set may be desired. For example, 2 sets (0:40 - 1:20 x 3). Sufficient rest must be provided to let the heart return to 120 beats per minute between sets. As the season progresses, the work intervals can be altered to meet the changing needs. For example, 2 sets (1:00 - 1:00 x 3) or 3 sets (0:30 - 0:20 x 3).

WORK INTERVAL DEVELOPMENT

In developing the interval training drills, the forwards, defensemen and goaltenders can work separately to the specified program or they can work together on similar drills. Naturally since the three groups have different skills some training should be done separately with each group.

If a coach is without help, he can give all three groups different drills but to the same ratio so that all will be working together and resting at the same time.

The coach in developing his drills should try to develop more than just stop and go skating drills. Sometimes, he can add skill techniques into the drill to help improve the skill level as well as the conditioning level. Stop and go drills with a puck will improve conditioning as well as puck control skills. As the name implies, it is interval training and with the definition of training, skill development should be coordinated with the conditioning process. The following sample drills show how conditioning and training are done with the same drill.

CHANGE OF DIRECTION ON THE WHISTLE

- A - start
- B - quick break forward
- C - stop on whistle and return as in phase D
- E - stop on whistle and quick break in opposite direction, F

Variations:

1. Have the player skate backwards for D

2. Have the player skate from the blue line to the other blue line and continue on in this pattern. This can also be done from the side boards to the other side boards.

3. Stickhandling with a puck will also develop skill as well as condition the body.

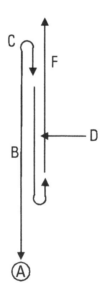

DEFENSEMAN'S CORNER DRILL

- A - start
- B - backward skate
- C - pivot to break into corner
- D - forward skate
- E - stop in corner
- F - quick break to start and repeat

This is a game condition drill as the defenseman will be required many times during a hockey game to execute this pattern.

This drill should also be worked to the other corner.

Variations:

1. Have the player pick up a puck at E and stickhandle to A

2. Have the player pick up a puck at E and make a pass to a player or a spot on the boards.

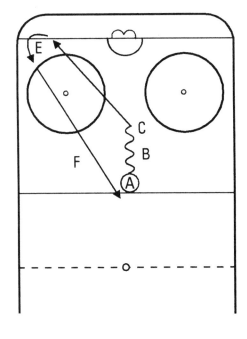

MIRROR DRILL

The player A moves to the arm signals of the coach. All directions should be utilized.

Variation: Have the players use a partner to give the mirror effect.

Goaltenders can use the following drills to set up interval training drills:

1. Mirror drills with a goalie partner

2. Up and down movements

3. Side to side movements.

4. Post to post movements

5. Out ten feet and back to net

6. Forward and backward skate with the defensemen.

7. Mirror drills with the defensemen.

Any maneuver or skill the goalie will be required to make in a game can be adapted to interval training. This also applies to the forwards and defensemen. A little practice with a new drill will soon give an idea as to how best to use the work/rest interval and ratio.

Some interval training can be done with partners. Skating drills such as partner pushing or pulling each other up and down the ice. Wrestling drills for balance and strength are also effective. Such drills are:

1. Partners facing each other holding one stick each with both hands and trying to wrestle the stick from the other without falling.
2. Using the same position, each tries to pull the other by backward skating.
3. Partners facing each other with each holding the other's arms and trying to force the other down.

WARM-UP, STRESS, AND FATIGUE

The athlete should have a warm-up before the interval training program. This warm-up is to help prevent strains, pulls and tearing of the muscle fibre. After the warm-up, stretching may be done. Do not use stretching as a warm-up. Get the body warm with light skating.

The work rate for the athlete's heart may reach 180 beats per minute and should not go over this level. Also, the heart rate must be at or lower than 140 beats per minute between sets. Pushing these limits will put too much strain on the athlete and as a result, the conditioning progress will be retarded. If the athlete cannot meet these objectives within the prescribed time limit then a longer rest may be required (increase the relief or rest interval). If this does not work, then the athlete may be suffering from exhaustion or some other medical problem.

Soreness is a signal for overstress and it must be guarded against. Acute and chronic soreness will require rest and or medical attention and the athlete should stop working out until it disappears.

DRY LAND PRESEASON PROGRAM

An interval training program can be set up for land conditioning. Basically it is much the same as the on-ice program previously outlined. Ratios, work load, rest intervals, etc. are manipulated in much the same way to receive a very desirable program. The following is a short sample:

2 sets (50 yards - 20 seconds x 10)

2 sets (440 yards - 2:00 minutes x 10)

1 set (880 yards - 4:00 minutes x 2)

1 880 yard light jog to cool down.

OVERALL CONCLUSIONS

In devising the program the following rules are important:

1. Do not start an exercise if the heart rate is above 140 beats per minute. If there is serious difficulty in achieving this level then cancel the workout. If the heart rate is excessive, well over the 180 limit then stop the exercise and rest.

2. Do not let the athlete become too exhausted; give him time to rest and recover. If necessary, the rest interval may have to be increased.

3. Excessive soreness must be treated or rested.

4. Heat prostration is a danger, and more likely in the dry land conditioning. Care must be taken during hot humid days. In some cases the cooler evening hours may be preferable for training.

5. Do not hesitate to let the players drink plenty of water and other liquids during the workouts. Restricting liquid intake can cause body dehydration with serious consequences.

6. Cool down after each workout. The conditioning program should provide the athletes with a chance to skate lightly or jog, to help prevent the build up of lactic acid in the body after heavy exercise.

3
Skating Drills

1. Laps
2. Laps with quick breaks between the blue lines
3. Stops and starts
4. Forward and backward skating with pivot
5. Change of direction
6. Forward and backward change of direction
7. Forward between blue lines and backward around corners
8. Sequence drill
9. Lateral backward skating
10. Single skating circle drill
11. Figure 8
12. Skating the square
13. Skating drills without lifting the feet
14. Stick jumping
15. Running on toes
16. Relay races
17. Three man relay
18. Three man race around the rink
19. Tandem drills

1. Laps

Forward and backward skating around the rink. Sometimes is a good idea to pull the net out a little from the crease area to give more room.

Coaching Notes: This is a warm-up drill and a conditioning drill the coach can control. Laps at the beginning of practice are for warm-ups. Laps later in the practice are conditioning drills as the intensity of the skating increases. The skating can be at full speed, three-quarters speed, half-speed, etc.

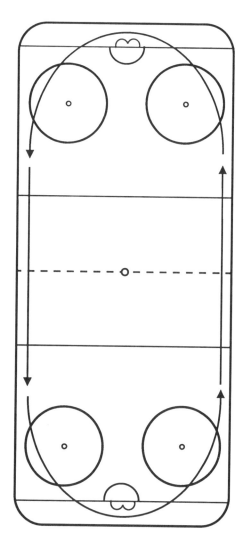

2. Laps with quick breaks between the blue lines

The players make a quick break between the blue lines and slow down around the corners.

Coaching Notes: Make sure the players are precise in their quick break. If the break is at the blue then the players must break at the blue line, not in front or after, but exactly at the blue line. This teaches the player discipline and precision. Breaking too soon or too late is carelessness and breeds an attitude of breaking when the players feels like it. In game situations, the quick break must be performed precisely when needed not when one feels like it.

Variations:

1. Players go slow between the blue lines and quick break around the corners.
2. Player takes a quick break of three or four strides everytime he hits a line on the ice.

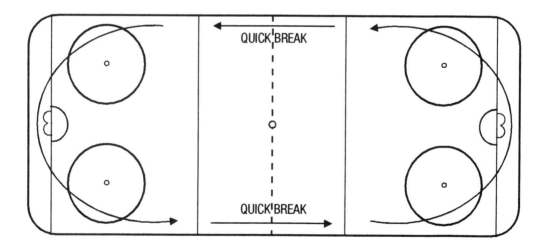

3. Stops and starts

The stops and starts can be made to various patterns governed by the whistle or ice markings.

The patterns can run lengthwise, sideways or from laps.

Coaching Notes: Hockey is stop and starts. The coach must demand quickness in execution. Slow or lazy stop and starts will carry over into games. Quick stop and starts in a game may mean gaining puck possession, covering a check, preventing a goal, or a hundred other factors that result in efficient play.

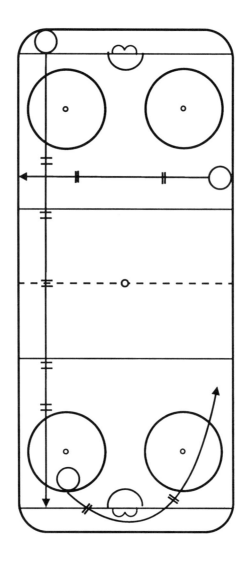

4. Forward and backward skating with pivot

Whistle or lines can signal various patterns of forward and backward skating.

Coaching Notes: Precision in executing the pivot at the proper time is important. Do not let the players be lazy in their timing of the pivot. Pivots must be executed on the whistle, no delays. Observe the footwork and balance of the players. Make sure they lift their feet. If their feet drag or twist on the ice then the pivot is improperly executed. If necessary, spend time on the pivot technique.

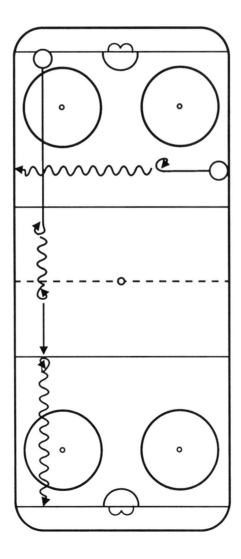

5. Change of direction

Changing directions can be signaled by the whistle or the ice markings. The skill can be lengthwise, sideways or in laps.

Coaching Notes: Again timing must be precise. Lazy habits or tendencies can not be tolerated. Check on the balance of the players and if the players outside leg is doing the majority of the stop. The inside leg rotates quickly for the next skating stride in the new direction.

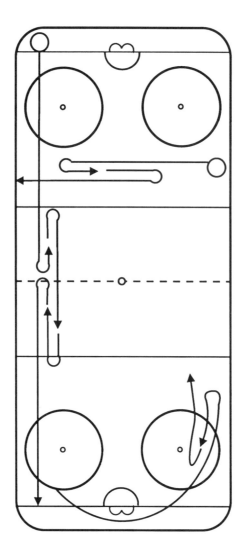

6. Forward and backward skating with change of direction

A whistle or a line can signal a change of forward skating to backward skating in the opposite direction, or vice versa.

Coaching Notes: Look for skill execution and timing.

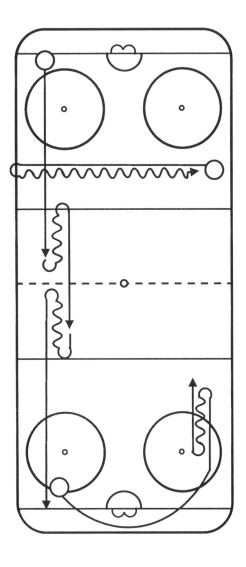

7. Forward skating between blue lines and backward skating around corners

This can also be done backward between the blue lines and forward around the corners.

Coaching Notes: Vary the speed of the skating, half-speed, three-quarters speed, and note the efficiency of the skating, pivoting, and rounding of the corners.

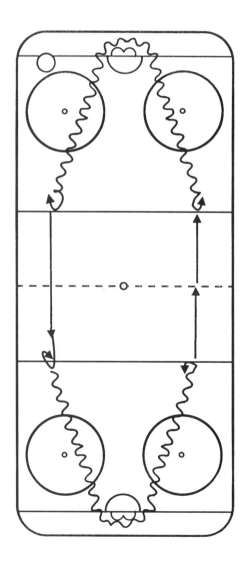

8. Sequence drill

Players skate to: the blue line and back, to the red line and back, to the far blue line and back, and then to the other end and back. This is one set. Skating can be forward or backward.

Coaching Notes: This is an excellent conditioning drill as well as a training drill if pucks are used for the players to stickhandle. Again, the players must change direction exactly on the lines (or on the whistle).

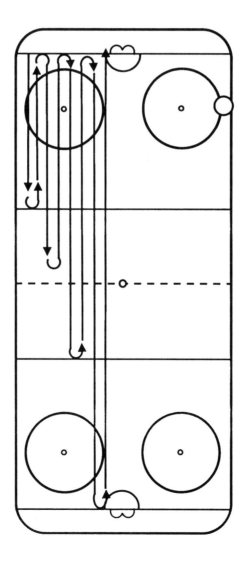

9. Lateral backward skating

The first player at the end starts skating backwards but moves to one side for about three strides and then back with three more strides to the other side. This side to side pattern is continued to the other end. The second player starts as soon as the first player has progressed a few feet from the boards. This individually delayed start continues down the line so that there is less chance of the players colliding or interfering with each other.

Coaching Notes: The player moves from side to side, but his chest remains pointing straight ahead. This is a good drill for defensemen as well as an overall agility drill.

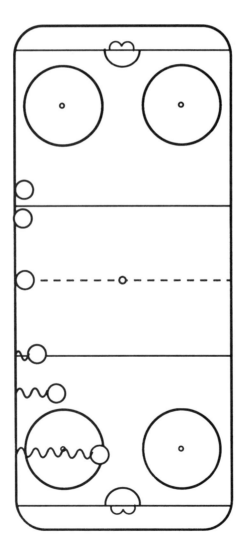

10. Single circle skating drill

The players spread out to all circles and skate the circle on commands of forward, backward and changing directions.

Coaching Notes: Look for balance and agility. If necessary, the crossover of the leg may have to be practiced more than planned.

Variation: Carry puck for stickhandling practice.

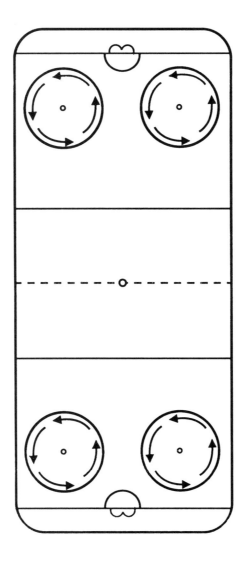

11. Figure "8"

Various patterns can be arranged to alter the size of the "8" or turns.

Coaching Notes: As during the circle skating drill, look for balance and agility. Good drill for stickhandling.

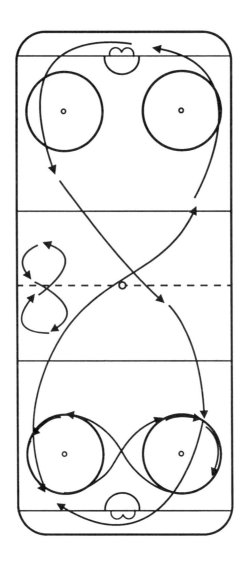

12. Skating the square

The players must make quick sharp turns. Lateral mobility can be emphasized on the blue and red lines by having the players move down the lines laterally.

Coaching Notes: When moving laterally, the players must keep their chest pointing straight ahead. Agility is critical in this drill.

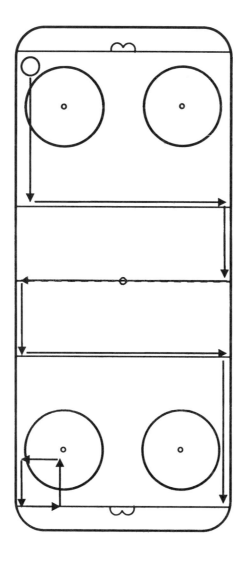

13. Skating drills without lifting feet

This is good for balance, strength, and agility.

Coaching Notes: Look for strong thrusting action.

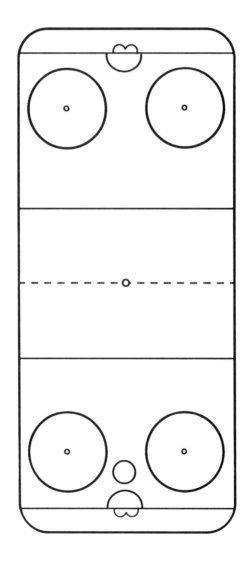

14. Stick jumping

Hockey sticks are placed horizontally above the ice on pylons or other some other means to give height. Some jumping skills are:

1. One foot take off
2. Two foot take off
3. Spin in the air
4. Land on one foot
5. Land and roll
6. Jump and land backward

Coaching Notes: The players must learn to balance on takeoff and landing. If necessary, show how the legs are used to cushion the landing.

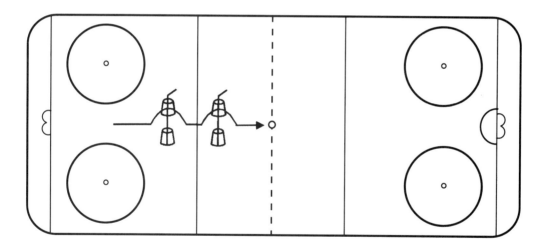

15. Running on toes

Lay hockey sticks on the ice so that the players can run on their toes with only one step between each stick. Sticks have to be fairly close together.

Coaching Notes: Be careful with this drill. If a player steps or lands on a hockey stick, the player can take a severe fall. Do not use this drill unless the players are dressed in full gear with helmets.

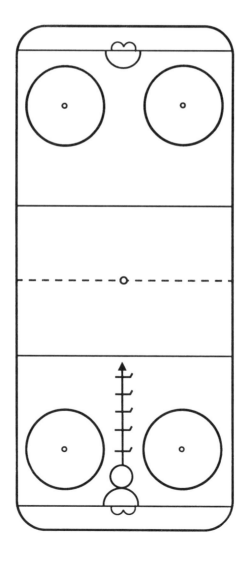

16. Relay races

Various skills can be emphasized in relay races.

Coaching Notes: Relay races can be excellent conditioning drills if there are not too many people standing around watching. Have small teams so there is more action. Relay races are usually lots of fun and give a friendly competition atmosphere.

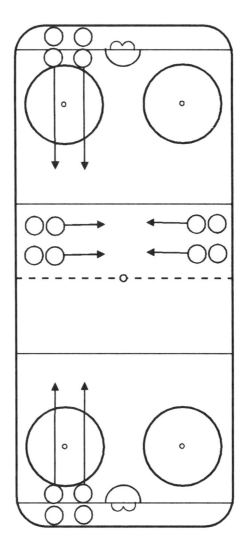

17. Three man relay

Player B starts and skates to A, player A skates to C and C skates to far boards to continue pattern.

Coaching Notes: Relay races with three men on a team give everyone plenty of action. With large team relays, a player has to wait too long for his turn. Small team relays are also excellent conditioning drills.

Variations:

1. Backward skating
2. Puck carry
3. Various skills can be used
4. Good conditioner

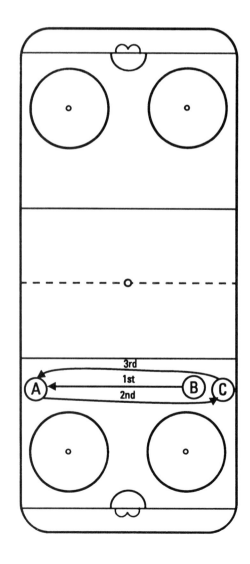

18. Three man race around the rink

Players in groups of threes race down the ice, around the net and back down the ice. Sometimes the last player has to go again with the next group.

Coaching Notes: This is a good conditioning drill, as well as a fun drill. Keep the players moving by sending the next three players before the other three finish their race.

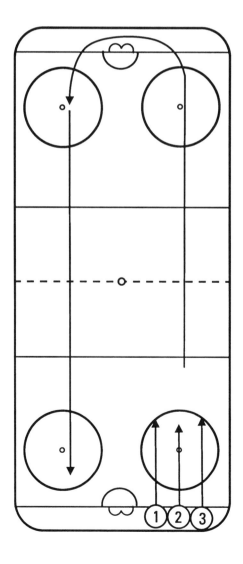

19. Tandem drills

Push — Two players facing each other hold each other's outstretched arms. One pushes while the other player gives resistance by using the snow plow with his skates.

Pull — Players face each other and hold the same hockey stick. One pulls the other with backward skating while the other gives resistance with the snow plow stop.

Wrestle — Players facing each other, hold arms and try to wrestle the other person down. This can also be done with each holding the same hockey stick.

Coaching Notes: On the wrestle drill, do not let the players continue to wrestle once the arms break their hold.

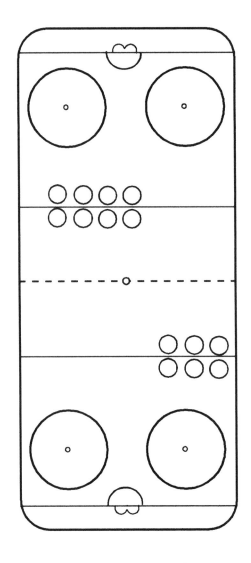

4
Puck Control Drills

20. Stationary stickhandling
21. Stickhandle weaves
22. Small area puck carry
23. Small area puck carry with two stealers
24. Foot control

20. Stationary stickhandling

Various formations can be used. The leader can have the players mirror him or he can call out instructions. To help youngsters keep their heads up the leader can hold his hand up for the player to watch and yell off the number of fingers he's holding up.

Coaching Notes: Have the players move the puck around their bodies by stickhandling in front and to each side. Also, the players should be able to move the puck in short sweeps of the stick and long sweeps of the stick. Check for hand position on the stick, and that the players keep their head up and the upper body erect and not slouched.

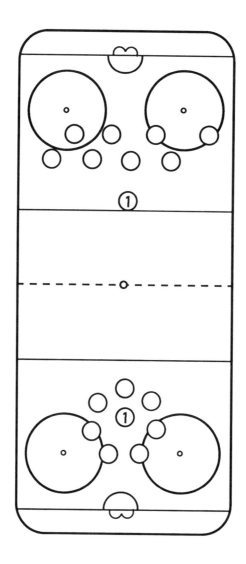

21. Stickhandle weaves

Pylons or sticks can be used to give various patterns or complexities.

1. Pattern A is a simple weave.

2. Pattern B is a simple weave except the pylons are spaced apart to give a wider weave.

3. Pattern C is a simple agility pattern. Naturally the coach can devise any pattern he desires.

Coaching Notes: Look for proper footwork as the player makes his weave. Is the body balanced on the turns? The players should be able to skate around each weave and not coast around the pylon.

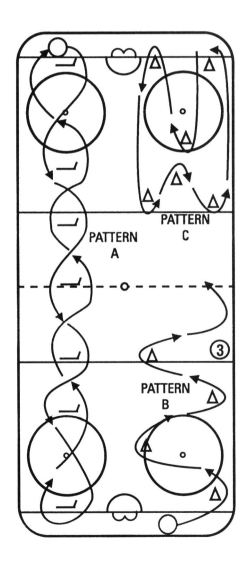

PATTERN A

PATTERN B

PATTERN C

22. Small area puck carry

Everyone has a puck and skates around a specific area. The area can be the end zones, between the blue lines, or between the red and blue line.

Coaching Notes: This is a good drill for agility skating and puck control. It is best if there are many players in a small area. Too much open area does not create congestion.

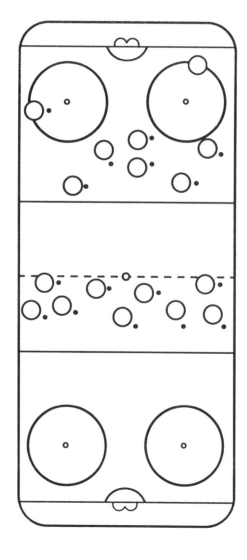

23. Small area puck carry with two stealers

Everyone has a puck except two players who attempt to steal one from someone else. The player who loses his puck then tries to steal one from someone else.

Coaching Notes: This is a good drill for agility skating, puck control, and puck protection. Hockey players must not only be able to control the puck, but they must also be able to protect the puck from the opposition. This drill can be used with or without body checking, although body checking will make the drill closer to game conditions.

Variation: Blow a whistle every so often and the players with no puck when the whistle blows must do something extra or humorous, like a lap around the ice, sing a song, twenty push-ups, etc.

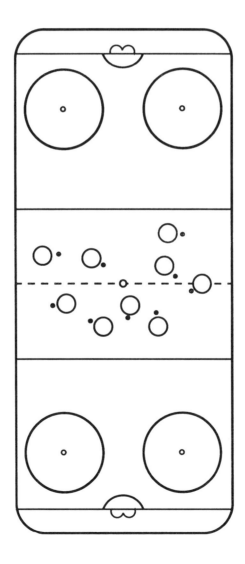

24. Foot control

Practice puck control with the feet. Many previous drills will help develop this skill.

Some skills to work on are:

1. Dribble the puck with the feet
2. Kick puck forward for stickhandling
3. Passing with the feet
4. Pass receiving with the feet

Coaching Notes: Puck control with the feet is a neglected skill. It is a skill that is extremely valuable when the puck is in the feet area, where it is difficult for the stick to be of much use. Hockey players with soccer skills will find puck control with the feet extremely useful and easy.

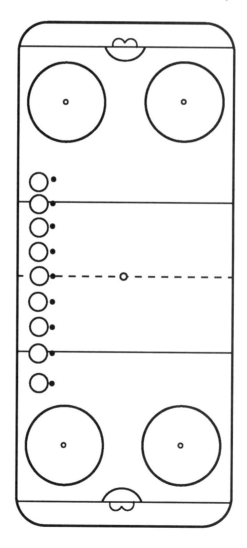

5
Passing and Shooting Drills

25. Stationary passing
26. Circle passing
27. Simple rink wide pass
28. Obstacle passing
29. Far winger offensive pass patterns
30. Pass out points
31. Assembly line pass and shot drill
32. Partner off the board passes
33. Off-the-boards pass for shot on goal
34. Off-the-boards pass to front of net
35. Corner off-the-boards pass to pointman for shot on goal
36. Behind the net off-the-boards pass and shot drill
37. Opposite way single rink wide pass
38. Opposite way double rink wide pass
39. 2-on-0 circular attack
40. Partner passing drill up and back

41. Four corner both ways passing drill
42. Drop pass on blue line
43. Partner pass back drill
44. The grapevine
45. Grapevine with 2-on-1 return
46. Give and go
47. Alternating multiple give and go
48. Give and go from corner for shot on goal
49. Center loop and pass drill
50. Long double loop, pass and shot drill
51. Breakout pass to far wing with return pass for shot
52. Long breakout pass
53. Half rink breakout pass
54. Wing's near corner breakout pass
55. Corner breakout pass to wing from defenseman
56. Corner breakout pass to wing by shooter from near corner
57. Corner breakout pass to wing by shooter from far corner

58. Whirlwind drill

59. Whirlwind 1-on-1

60. Whirlwind with pass to point

61. Wing to looping center, pass and shot drill

62. Double defenseman breakout pass to center

63. Double defensemen breakout pass to center with 2-on-1 attack

64. Stationary shooting

65. Shooting in stride

66. Cuts for shots on goal

67. Single rapid fire shooting

68. Back and forth puck pickup for shot on goal

69. Flip shot practice drill

70. Scattered shooting drill

71. Empty net shooting practice

72. Penalty shot individual

73. Penalty shooting

74. Shooting rolling or bouncing puck

75. Give and go from corner with three different lineups

76. Corner pass out with check

77. Double shot drill

78. Playing puck rounding boards behind the net

79. Corner break in with check

80. Out of corner loop for shot on goal

81. Tip-ins

82. Stationary shooting with single tip-ins

83. Stationary shooting with single tip-ins and check

84. Stationary shooting with double tip-ins and check

85. One puck rebounds

86. Simulated double rebound shooting

25. Stationary passing

Partners pass back and forth over different distances. Forehand and backhand passing must be practiced.

Coaching Notes: This drill is for basic practice of the pass. It also gives the coach a chance to observe mechanics. Check that the players are pushing the stick straight to the target with no flipping or twisting of the stick blade. Be sure that the players are in balance and not falling away from the pass. The players must also be looking at the target. The pass receiver must place his stick on the ice to give the passer a target as well as telling the passer where he wants the puck.

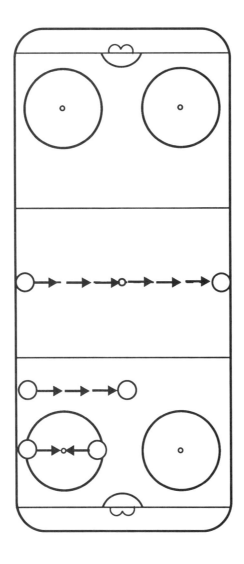

26. Circle passing

Stationary: Players pass around one puck. More pucks are gradually added.

Rotary: Players skate in a circle and pass a puck around. More pucks are gradually added.

Emphasis can be put on forehand and backhand passing and pass receiving. Passes can be made in circular patterns of clockwise or counterclockwise or in a random fashion of passing to anyone.

Coaching Notes: This drill gives variety to the pass in that the pass receiver will not always be at right angles to the pass as in drill number 25. The pass receiver must place his stick on the ice where he wants the puck. The stick blade becomes a target for the passer.

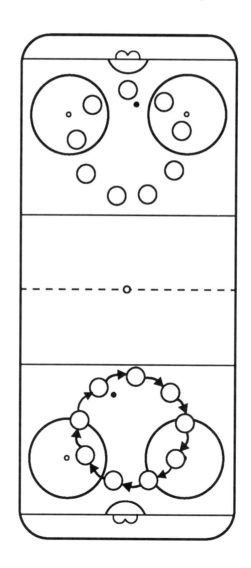

27. Simple rink-wide passes

Players 1 and A advance up the ice using rink-wide passes.

Coaching Notes: This drill involves movement by the passer and pass receiver for practice in leading the pass receiver. If the players are having difficulty completing the passes then a shorter pass can be utilized. Be sure the players put their stick on the ice to give the passer a target. Many players skate with their hockey stick swinging back and forth. This skating action makes it difficult for the passer to have a good target.

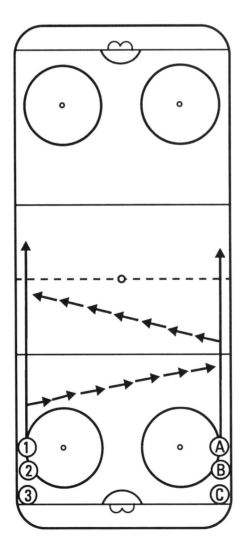

28. Obstacle passing

Players 1 and 2 advance by passing between the sticks. A and B advance by passing over the sticks. Forehand and backhand passes must be practiced.

Coaching Notes: This is an excellent drill to develop precision in passing. The openings between the sticks can be varied to smaller spaces as skill level increases. As skill increases, the speed of the skaters will also increase. As speed increases and the spaces get smaller, the players' skill in pass receiving and passing becomes quicker and quicker. In time, the players should be able to receive the pass and give the return pass in one continuous quick motion.

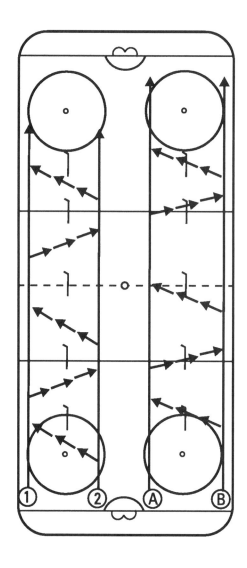

29. Far winger offensive pass patterns

Player 1 passes to 2 from the corner. A passes to B by using the boards behind the goal net.

Coaching Notes: In game conditions, the pass to the far winger is often an excellent scoring opportunity. The passing off the boards is also a chance to learn the angles of the puck bouncing off the boards. Passing accurately off the boards is extremely valuable during games.

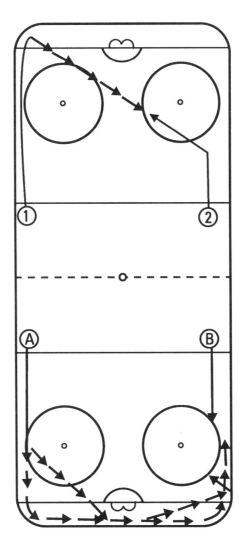

30. Pass out points

Passes for shots on goal should be made from all possible points such as A, B, C, D, and E.

Coaching Notes: Passes for shots on goal will come from many positions. Players must learn to receive a pass from any angle and get the shot away on goal as quickly as possible.

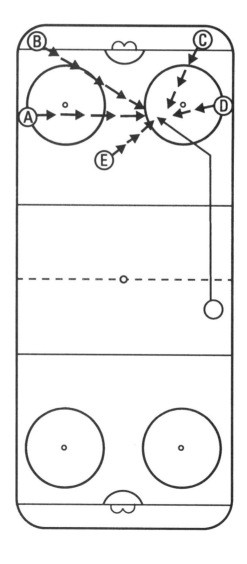

31. Assembly line pass and shot drill

Player 1 passes puck to 2 who continues it along the pattern to 5 for the shot on goal. As soon as 2 releases the puck, 1 passes another puck to 2. The object is to keep as many pucks as possible moving as quickly as possible, much like a rapid assembly line.

Coaching Notes: This drill practices quick puck movement for a shot on goal. Be sure the passes are flat on the ice with no bouncing. A bad pass or bounce will break the sequence of passes.

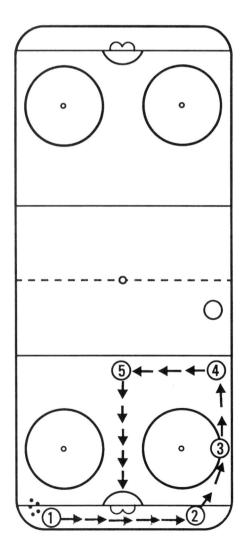

32. Partner off-the-boards passes

Player B passes the puck off-the-boards to A and then breaks ahead of A to receive A's off-the-boards pass.

Coaching Notes: The boards are often referred to as an extra man. Naturally, this is true only if the boards and passes off the boards are accurate. This drill gives practice in using boards to pass to a teammate or to pass to yourself to get around an opponent. In time, the players should be able to read the angles on pucks when they are bouncing off the boards.

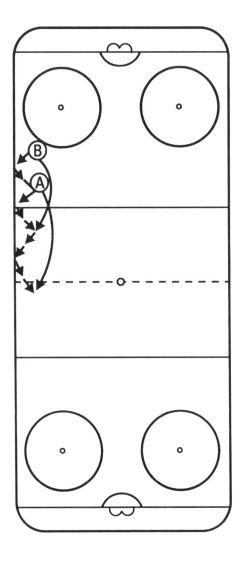

33. Off-the-boards pass for shot on goal

Player 1 passes off-the-boards to 2 who attacks goal. 1 follows up for rebound.

Coaching Notes: This off-the-boards pass is an excellent method for passing to a teammate when an opposing player blocks a direct pass. The passer must learn to lead the pass receiver as well as how hard to make the pass. The pass receiver must learn to read the deflection off the boards and how to pace his speed to the speed of the puck off the boards.

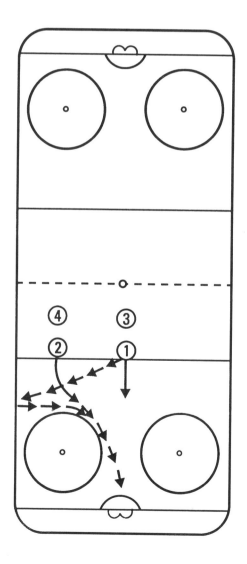

34. Off-the-boards pass to front of net

If the boards are lively at ice level, the boards can be an effective method of getting the puck in front of the goal, especially if 2's direct passing lane is blocked by A.

Coaching Notes: This is a game condition drill. Player 1 must always be alert for this type of pass from 2. Player 2 should also practice the bounce from the corner as it is very difficult – but effective – to read the angle off the rounded corner.

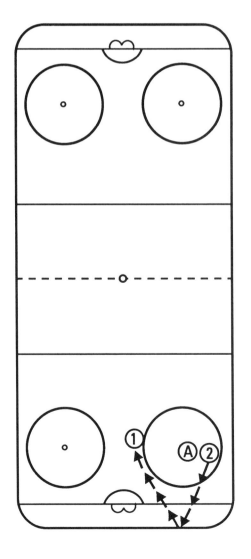

35. Corner off-the-boards pass to pointman (defenseman) for shot on goal.

Player A passes the puck off-the-boards to 1, a defenseman, for a shot on goal.

Coaching Notes: This drill is another variation on the off-the-boards pass for shots on goal. Emphasize quickness in shot execution. The players must get the shot away on goal quickly whether the puck is flat on the ice, on its edge, or even bouncing.

Variations:

1. Bang the puck off-the-boards at various speeds and heights so that sometimes 1 will have to block the puck to stop it from getting by him so he can play the shot on goal.

2. Bounce puck at boards near 1 so he must play the jammed puck against the boards.

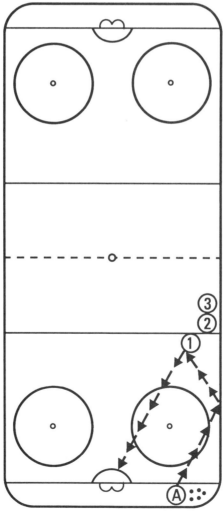

36. Behind the net off-the-boards pass and shot drill

Player 1 passes to A off-the-boards behind the net. A on receiving the pass relays it to 1 who is now in front of the net for a shot on goal.

Coaching Notes: Emphasize quickness in getting the shot away on goal. This type of pass and shot on goal will occur many times during a game.

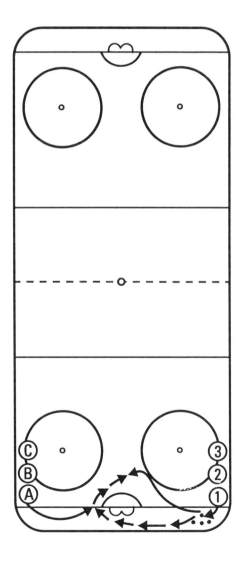

37. Opposite way single rink-wide pass

Players 1 and A skate and pass to each other and continue to goal for a shot.

Coaching Notes: This is an excellent drill in learning to lead the pass receiver. Keep the players moving quickly.

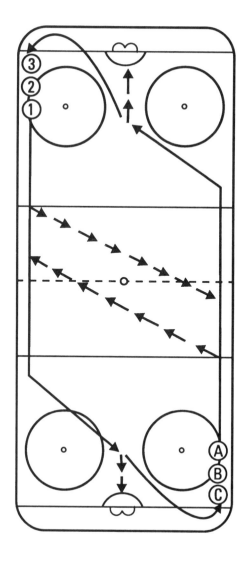

38. Opposite way double rink-wide pass

Players 1 and A exchange (pass to each other) passes at blue line. Player 1 continues to next blue line where he will exchange passes with B before shooting on net.

Coaching Notes: This drill is a progression from the opposite way single rink-wide pass.

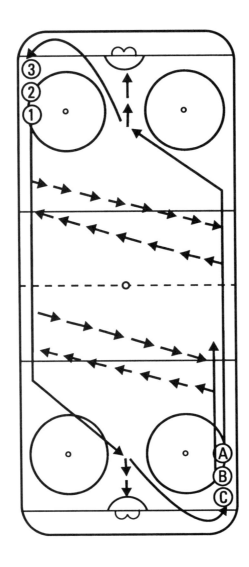

39. 2-on-0 circular drill

Player 1 passes to 2 and they both attack the goal. 2 shoots and 1 plays the rebound. 2 continues to the end of the next line while 1 continues circular pattern to take pass from A. Player A is now the rebounder for 1's shot on goal.

Rule: after playing rebound, player breaks for pass and shot on goal; after shooting. The player goes to end of next line.

Coaching Notes: This is an excellent conditioning and training drill. Skating, passing and shooting are emphasized. Keep this drill moving quickly with lots of snap and energy.

Variations:

1. Several units can be put in motion at the same time.

2. 2-on-1 can be used with this pattern.

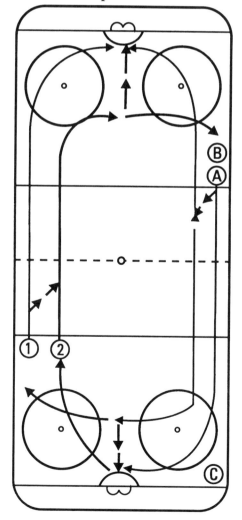

40. Partner passing drill up and back

Player 1 and A advance up the ice, close together, passing with short quick passes. At the end they loop around and come back wide with rink-wide passes.

When 1 and A reach the red line, 2 and B begin their passing. Players must be alert so as not to run into each other or pass into a player.

Coaching Notes: Excellent passing and skating drill. Develops short and long passes and forces the players to be alert so they do not run into each other.

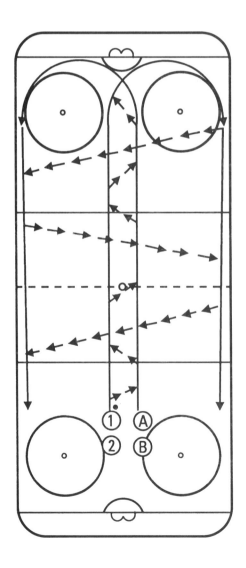

41. Four corner both ways passing drill

Players 1 and 2 using rink-wide passes attack the far goal as A and B attack the other goal. A and B must move to the center area so as not to collide with 1 and 2.

Coaching Notes: Excellent short and long passing drill. Players must be alert.

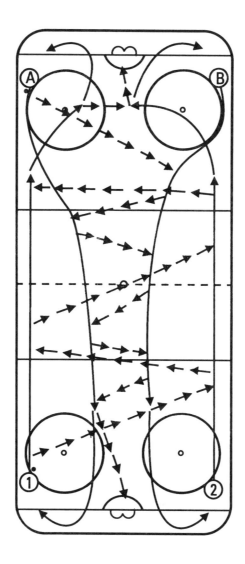

42. Drop pass on blue line

Player 1 skating along boards makes drop on the blue line. Puck must remain on the blue line.

Pass back to blue line: Player A skates over blue line and passes back to blue line and tries to have puck stop sliding on the blue line. The coach can put his stick in position as a target for the shooter.

Coaching Notes: The puck must be left or dropped on the blue line. Do not accept being close, the puck must be on the line. This accuracy is important in games as an accurate drop facilitates puck control for the teammate. The pass back must also have accuracy.

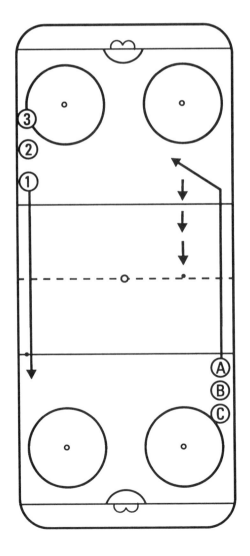

43. Partner pass back drill

Player A carries the puck in and executes pass back with 1.

Coaching Notes: Emphasize accuracy not only in passing but in player movement. Timing is extremely important as the passer and pass receiver must learn to pace themselves so that they will be properly positioned for the pass and shot on goal.

Variations:

1. This can also be done as a 2-on-1.

2. Instead of a pass back it can be a drop pass (partner drop pass play).

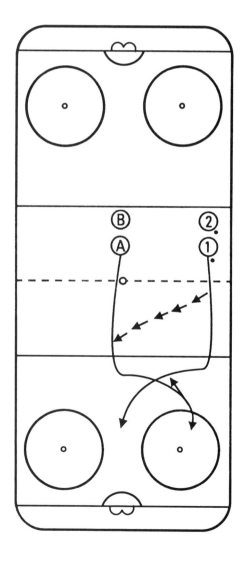

44. Grapevine

Player B passes to C and goes behind him to become wing. Player C takes pass and cuts to the center and passes to A; then goes behind A to wing position. A takes pass and cuts to center and passes to B, etc.

Rules:

1. Pass to wing, skate behind pass receiver to become wing.

2. Pass receiver cuts to center passes to wing and repeats rule 1.

Coaching Notes: This is a good skating and passing drill, but not exactly a game situation drill as the players are continually moving away from their wings or center position.

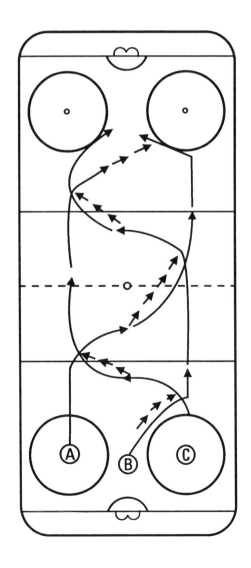

45. Grapevine with 2-on-1 return

Players A, B and C do the grapevine up the ice. On the attack on goal, the player closest to the blue line becomes the defenseman, while the two deepest players become forwards for the 2-on-1.

Coaching Notes: A variation of the grapevine to give practice for the attack on goal.

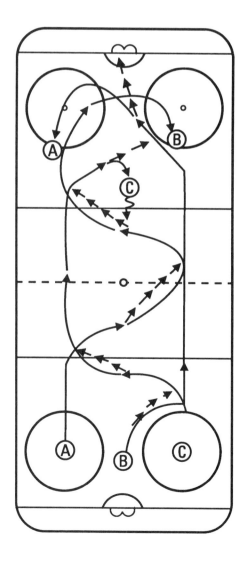

46. Give and go

Single—Player 1 passes to A, takes the return pass and continues on for a play on goal.

Double — Player 5 passes to B and C on his way to the goal.

Coaching Notes: Both drills are excellent warm-up drills as they are simple, effective, and involve skating, passing, and shooting.

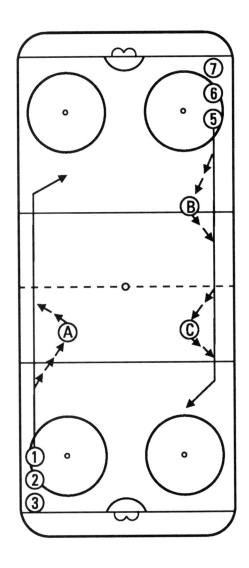

47. Alternating multiple give and go

Player A advances straight up the ice to far goal by passing the puck to 1, 2, 3, and 4. Fewer or more pass receivers may be used if desired.

Coaching Notes: Excellent drill for taking and giving passes on the forehand and backhand. Quickness in executing the pass is also essential.

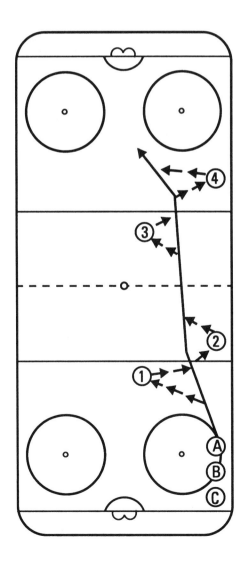

48. Give and go from corner for shot on goal

Player A passes to D and takes the return pass for shot on goal.

Coaching Notes: Good drill for quickness in pass receiving and shooting. Emphasize the receiving of the pass and the shot in one continuous motion. Do not let the shooter adjust the puck or take an extra stickhandle to get the shot away.

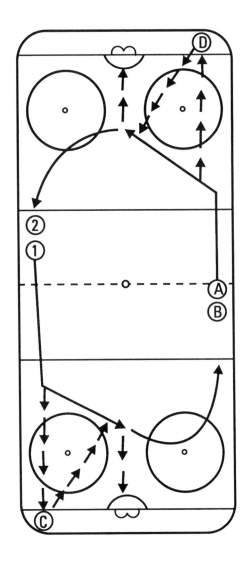

49. Center loop and pass drill

Player 1 loops into the end zone, takes a pass and attacks the far goal. 1 then goes to the corner to pass out to the next player. A repeats the same action as player 1 for action on both goals.

Coaching Notes: The pass receiver skates in a looping action similar to the action in a breakout play.

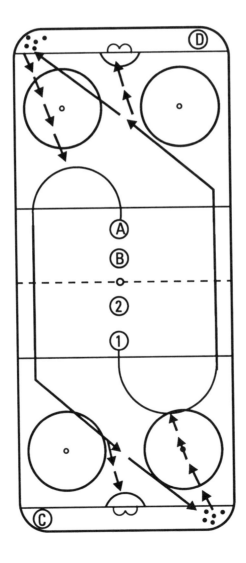

50. Long double loop, pass and shot drill

Player 1 and A skate along the boards to the far blue line and then loop and return to the near blue line to receive a breakout pass. On receiving the pass, 1 and A make a quick turn for a shot on the far goal. After their shot on goal, player 1 and A pass out to 2 and B from the corner.

Coaching Notes: Similar to drill number 49, but this drill involves more action and more player movement.

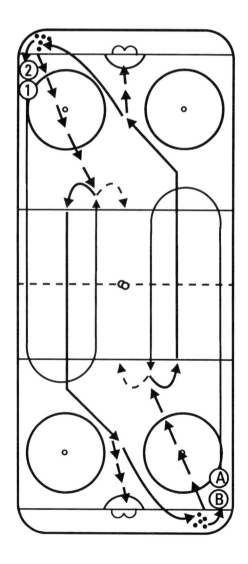

51. Breakout pass to far wing with return pass for shot

Player 1 passes to 2 with 2 passing to 3 who breaks up the ice and gives a pass to 4 for a shot on goal.

Coaching Notes: Similar to drill number 31, this drill also gives the wing practice in quick breaking on receiving a pass. This drill can be done at both ends of the ice for more player involvement.

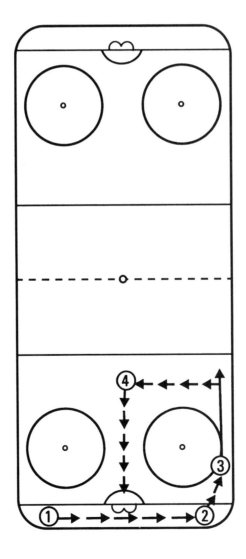

52. Long breakout pass

The defensemen alternate passes and hit the winger with a long pass.

Coaching Notes: This pass may not be used very much during a game, but it should be practiced as it can be an extremely effective breakout, often leading to a break-a-way.

Variation: Place a defenseman on the point to give some resistance.

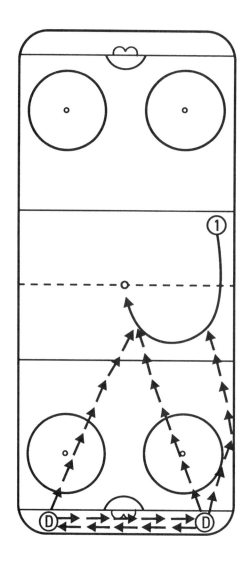

53. Half rink breakout pass

Player D passes to 1 breaking along boards who in turn relays puck to A who is looping into center.

Coaching Notes: This is a breakout play passing combination that is very similar to a game situation. Timing is extremely important.

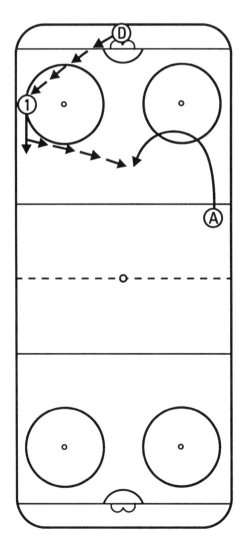

54. Wing's near corner breakout pass

Players 1 and 3 skate in to receive the breakout pass. With a quick turn they attack the far goal, after which they go into the corner to pass out to the next player.

Coaching Notes: Good drill for the winger breakout play. Timing and precision must be emphasized.

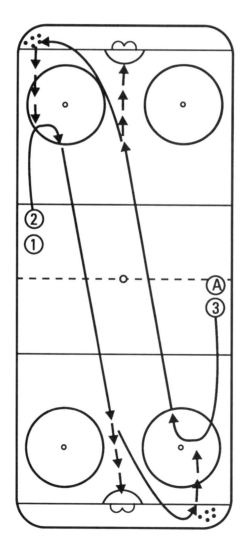

55. Corner Breakout pass to wing from defenseman

Player 1 skates towards corner to receive breakout pass from D1. A does the same on the other half of the ice.

Coaching Notes: Similar to drill number 54 except that the pass out is done by a defenseman.

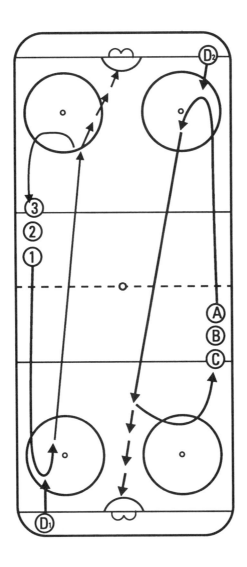

56. Corner breakout pass to wing by shooter from the near corner

Player 1 skates in for the breakout pass. 1 takes shot at far goal and then passes to B from the near corner. Player 1 then returns to the end of his line.

Coaching Notes: Similar to drill number 55 and 54 with the shooter making the pass-out to the next shooter.

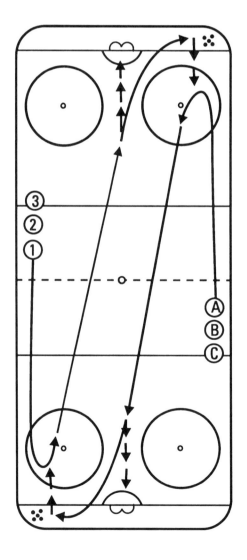

57. Corner breakout pass to wing by shooter from the far corner

Player 1 skates in for breakout pass from far corner. After shooting 1 passes out to B and then returns to end of line.

Coaching Notes: The pass from the far corner is a valuable pass during games. This type of pass can be dangerous as the pass can be cut off by the opposition. This pass should only be used when no danger of the cutoff is present. The pass must be practiced as it can be an excellent breakout pass.

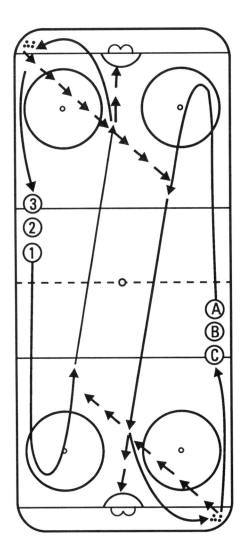

58. Whirlwind drill

Player 1 skates toward the net, receives a pass and shoots on goal. After shooting, 1 goes to the corner to pass out to the next player and then moves on to the end of the line.

Coaching Notes: This is an excellent skating, passing, shooting, and conditioning drill. The players must be kept moving quickly to live up to the name of the drill.

Variations:

1. Player A picks up the puck in the corner and skates hard to the blue line and then passes to 8 skating towards the goal.

2. A player may be added to harass the player in the corner.

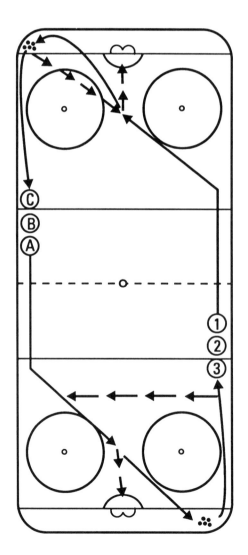

59. Whirlwind 1-on-1

A defenseman is added to the whirlwind drill to give a 1-on-1 situation to the player attacking the goal.

Coaching Notes: By adding a defenseman, the drill becomes a game situation drill.

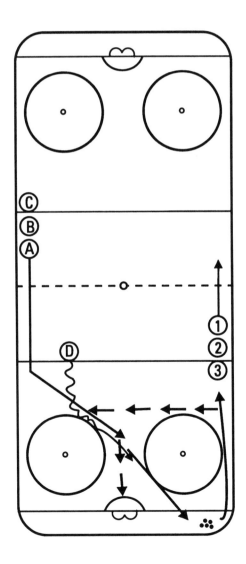

60. Whirlwind with pass to point

Player 1 breaks for the goal and receives a pass from 4 for a shot on goal. After shooting, 1 passes to 4 who passes to 2 breaking to the goal. 4 then goes to the end of the line behind C while 1 moves up to 4's position as the point.

Coaching Notes: A variation to the whirlwind drill that involves more passing accuracy and precision movement.

Variation: A defenseman D can be used to give a 1-on-1 situation (Whirlwind with a pass to point and a 1-on-1).

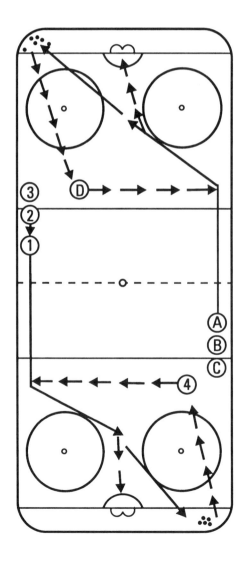

61. Wing to looping center, pass and shot drill

Player A and 1 loop into center ice area, take pass from B and 2 respectively, and break for shot on goal.

With good timing, this drill can put three, four or more players in motion, to give quick action on goal as well as discipline in movement and timing.

Coaching Notes: Good drill for player involvement as players must move quickly. Timing of the pass and pass receiver must be accurate.

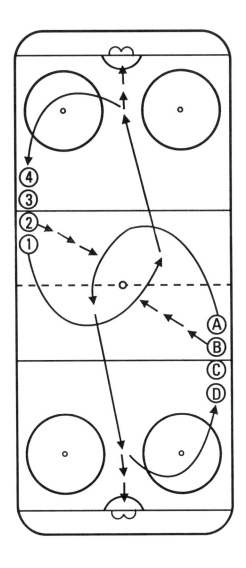

62. Double defensemen breakout pass to center

Player D1 passes, while skating backwards, to D2 who in turn relays it to player 1. At the other end, D3 and D4 do the same thing with A. Like the wing to looping center pass, more players can be put into motion.

Coaching Notes: Excellent drill for player involvement as almost everyone is involved. This can be an excellent conditioning drill under game situations. Timing of player movement and passing is crucial in this drill. The looping center must receive the pass at the beginning of his loop or during the loop. Too late a pass and the center is looking over his back for the pass. This you definitely do not want.

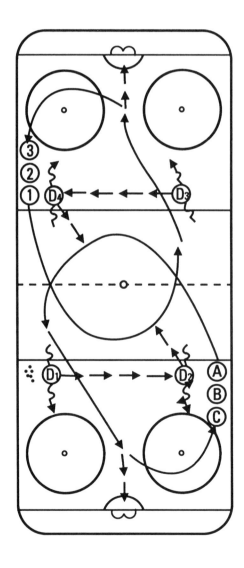

63. Double defensemen breakout pass to center with a 2-on-1 attack

Player A and 1 start their loop. Player 2 joins A for 2-on-1 against D3. Player B joins 1 for 2-on-1 against D1, and players C and 3 loop for their breakout pass to continue drill.

Coaching Notes: This drill is very close to game situations. Again, timing is essential, and players must be alert to prevent collisions.

Variations:

1. A 2-on-0 situation: The same drill except no defensemen are involved in attack.

2. A defenseman D5 can be placed between D1 and D2 and D6 can be placed between D3 and D4 to play the 2-on-1.

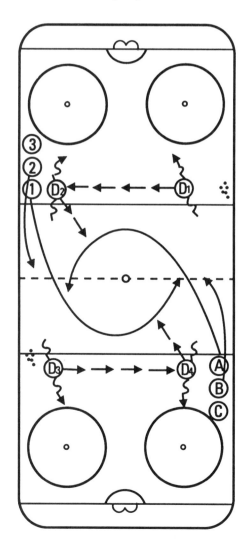

64. Stationary shooting

Players may use the straight line or semicircle pattern for shooting. Shots can be in sequence or alternating from end to end.

Coaching Notes: This is a shooting drill for the goaltender. It is also a good time to work on special moves by the goaltender and techniques/mechanics by the shooter. Various types of shots by forehand and backhand must be practiced for benefit to the shooters and the goaltenders.

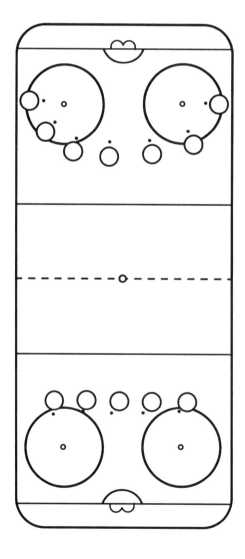

65. Shooting in Stride

Work on this through various shooting drills. It is also possible to have the players skate towards the boards and shoot in stride.

Coaching Notes: Players must learn to shoot in stride so that the puck is shot on goal quickly with no warning to the goaltender. Too often shooters telegraph their shots by adjusting their feet, coasting, extra stickhandling, or dropping their head or upper body. These adjustments are a key to the goaltender in reading the shot.

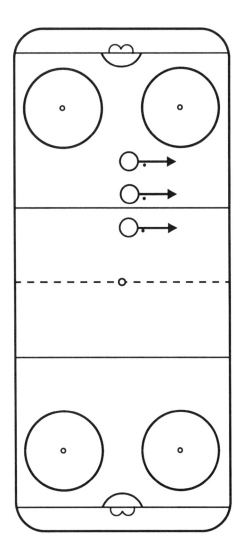

66. Cuts for shots on goal

Players breaking for the net cut towards the goal at the pylons placed in various positions.

Coaching Notes: Players must learn to make a cut to the goal net from various positions. Players carelessly cutting to the net usually make the cut too soon and deceive no one.

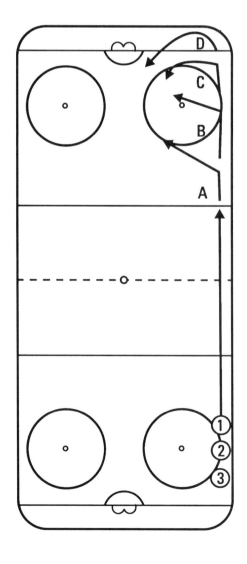

67. Single rapid fire shooting

Pucks are lined up and a player A goes down the line shooting each puck as quickly as possible. Pucks can be lined in various patterns.

Coaching Notes: These are quick reaction drills not only for the shooter but also for the goaltender. The players must practice balance and efficiency of movement.

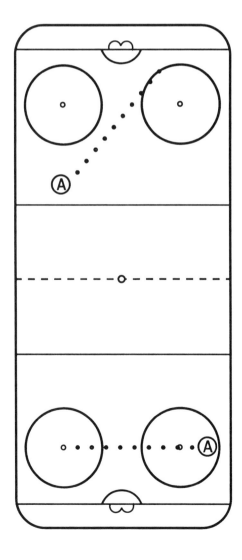

68. Back and forth puck pick up for shot on goal

Player A, picking up puck at blue line, moves in for shot on goal. After shooting, A skates back to get another puck and repeats drill until all the pucks are played. Players can be timed for speed.

Coaching Notes: This is a reaction drill that involves skating and shooting. This is a demanding drill and can be excellent for conditioning.

Variation: The player dekes the goalie instead of shooting

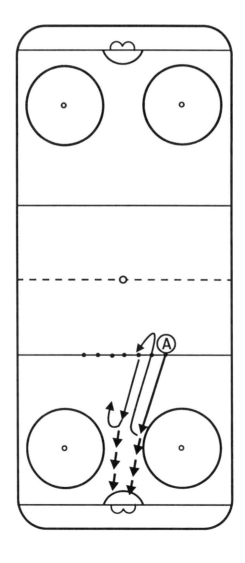

69. Flip shot practice drill

Players 1 and A skate to the blue line or red line and flip the puck at the goalie so that it takes an unpredictable bounce in front of the goal.

Coaching Notes: Good drill for goaltenders in playing the crazy bouncing puck. Also good for the shooters in practicing the clearing pass.

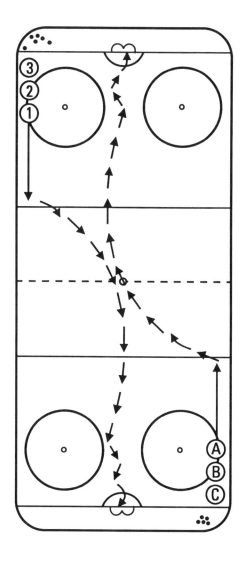

70. Scattered shooting drill

Pucks are scattered in end zone. The shooter must shoot all pucks as quickly as possible. This drill can be timed.

Coaching Notes: Another conditioning and training drill. Very good for goaltenders and shooters in getting the puck away on goal quickly.

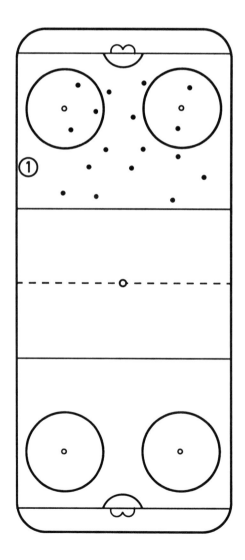

71. Empty net shooting practice

The players skate around the goal net and try to score in the empty net at the other end of the ice.

Coaching Notes: This may seem easy. Actually, it is difficult to hit an open net at the far end of the rink. This is a game situation drill when the opposition pulls their goalie. Resistance to the empty net shot can be provided by having an attacker pressure A. This can be a fun drill with the players.

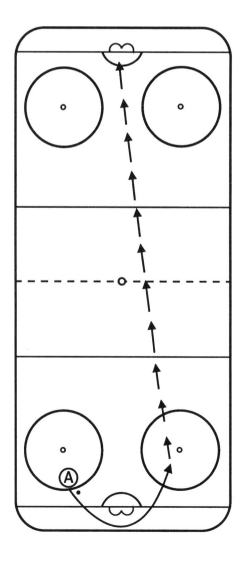

72. Penalty shot individual

Player 1 and A advance for their play on goal. After the goal attack they return to the other line for a play on the other goalie.

Coaching Notes: This is a pressure situation drill for the shooter and the goaltender. This can also be a "fun" drill as the players will enjoy the competition.

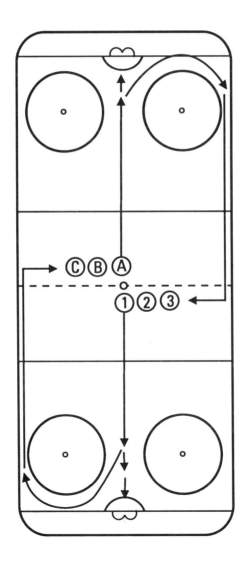

73. Penalty shooting

Individual — Each player takes his turn on the penalty shot with the winner being the one who scores the most out of so many shots or the one left who hasn't missed scoring (single elimination).

Team — Two teams are formed and the team scoring the most goals wins.

Coaching Notes: A fun but highly effective drill for pressure situations.

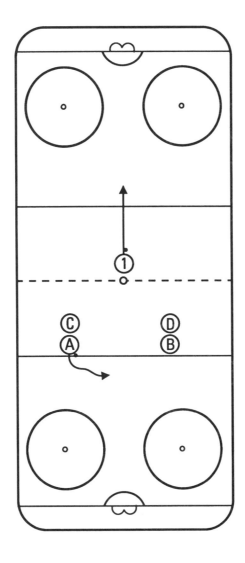

74. Shooting rolling or bouncing puck

The puck is rolled or bounced to player 1 for a shot on goal. Usually it is best to throw puck by hand to achieve a good roll or bounce.

Coaching Notes: Game situations involve many opportunities to shoot a rolling or bouncing puck on goal. In most cases, wrist action will cause the puck to flip over the stick blade. Usually, it is best to shoot the puck with a stiff wrist action.

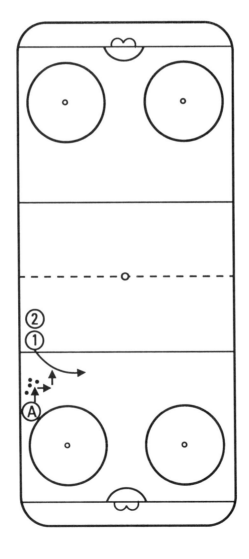

75. Give and go from corner with three different lineups

Player 1 passes to A and breaks for the net. A returns the pass to 1 who takes his shot on goal and then waits in position B for his next turn. After shooting from B, 1 lines up at position C.

Coaching Notes: This is a simple give and go from the corner to give a game situation. Emphasis should be on shooting in stride and as quickly as possible.

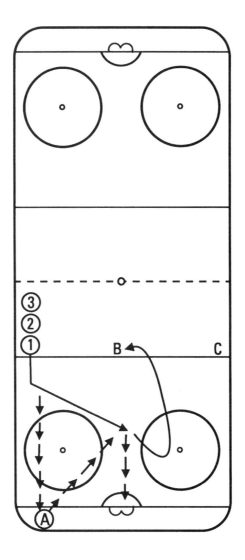

76. Corner pass out with check

Player 2 passes to 1 for a shot on goal. A, the defenseman, checks 1.

Coaching Notes: This is a pressure shot drill. The shooter is under pressure by the defender A. Excellent drill for practice in the scramble situations that occur in front of the goal net. The passer, shooter, and defender all receive game situation practice.

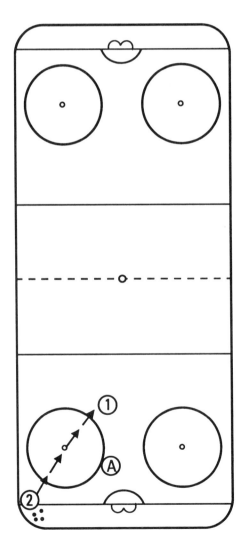

77. Double shot drill

Player 1 uses the give and go with A and then skates over the blue line and shoots on goal. After shooting he continues breaking for the goal to receive a pass for another shot on goal.

Coaching Notes: The shots must be executed quickly and efficiently so that both shots will be performed. This drill helps the shooter to continue to the goal for another shot or rebound.

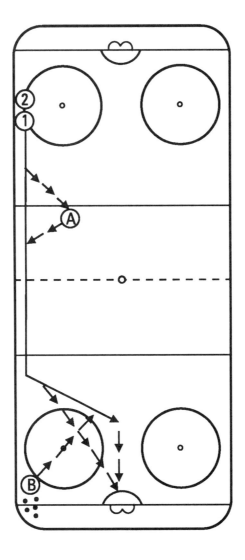

78. Playing the puck rounding boards behind the net

Player A shoots the puck off-the-boards or along the boards to the far defenseman B for a shot on goal.

Coaching Notes: The pass by A to B occurs often during a game. Player B, usually a defenseman, must learn to take the pass off the boards. Sometimes the puck is along the ice or higher on the boards. If the puck is off the ice, player B may have to block the puck with his body. When the puck is rounded off the boards, the puck is spinning extremely fast and this spin action creates difficulty in controlling the pass. The pass receiver must be alert to this spinning action of the puck.

Variation: Player B stops puck and passes to C for the shot on goal.

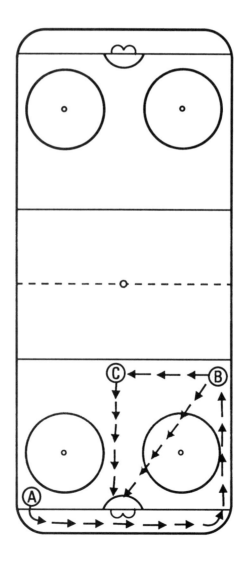

79. Corner break in with check

Player A, the puck carrier, breaks in around the pylon for a scoring attempt. 1 tries to prevent A's attack.

Coaching Notes: An excellent drill to up a scoring opportunity from the corner. Good for the goaltender playing the shot on goal while the shooter is being hassled.

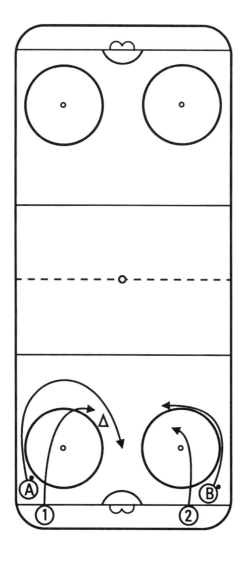

80. Out of corner loop for shot on goal

Players 1 and B alternate skating around the coach for shot on goal. Speed of play and shot rapidity can vary.

Coaching Notes: A simple drill for shooters but good for the goaltenders. The coach is in position to analyze the shooting and the goaltender's action.

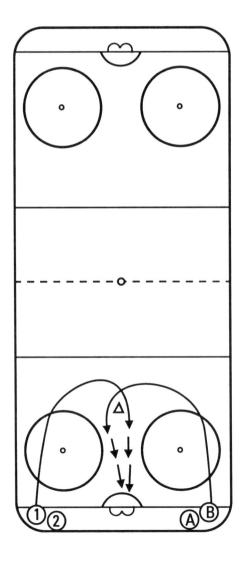

81. Tip-ins

Stationary—Players form a semicircle pattern with A in front of the goal for the tip-ins.

Dual—1 passes to 2 and then breaks to the front of the goal for a tip-in.

Coaching Notes: Excellent drill for goaltenders as a goaltender is faced with so many tip-in and deflected shots. Tip-ins and deflections are difficult to execute. Practice is essential to this skill. The dual drill is a game situation as player 1 breaks for the goal after making his pass.

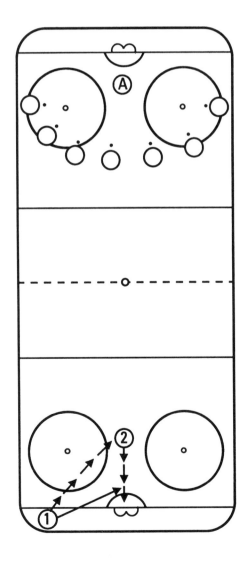

82. Stationary shooting with single tip-ins

Players 1 through 6 take turns shooting on goal. Player 7 tips, screens, or rebounds shots. Shooting can be in order or alternate from end to end (1 then 6, then 2, then 5, etc.).

Coaching Notes: Simple tip-in drill. Often a good drill to use between two demanding drills to give a little change of pace or rest.

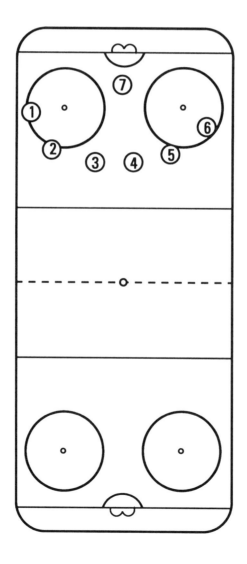

83. Stationary shooting with single tip-ins and check

Players 1 through 6 shoot on goal while 7 tips, screens, or rebounds shots. A checks 7.

Coaching Notes: Player A provides additional goal protection as well as pressuring 7 for the tip-ins. This drill is excellent for the goaltender as he learns and practices reading the puck with all the action in front of him.

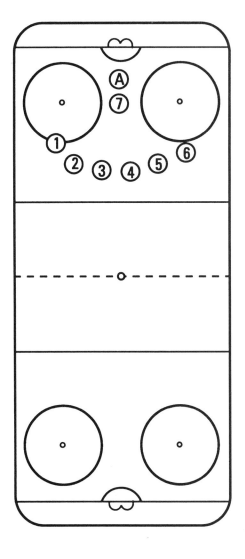

84. Stationary shooting with double tip-ins and check

Players 1 through 6 shoot on goal while 7 and 8 tip, screen or rebound shots. A checks player playing the puck. Players alternate shooting to give A lots of movement and agility, or each shooter can have a number and the coach calls out the shooter by number. This drill can be done with two checks, 1-on-7 and 1-on-8.

Coaching Notes: Plenty of action for the goaltender and the defender A. Player A tries to stop 7 and 8 from deflecting the puck as well as preventing himself from screening the goaltender. This is an excellent goal mouth scramble action.

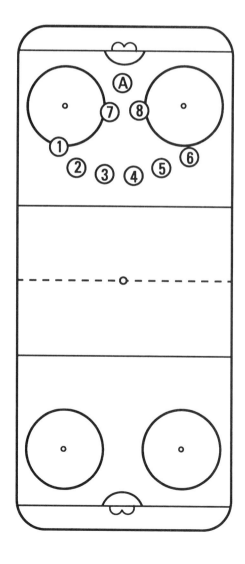

85. One puck rebound

Player 1 shoots while 2 and 3 play the rebound.

Coaching Notes: Good drill for goaltenders to practice playing the first shot and then the rebounds. Also, a good drill for the attackers in developing quickness of rebound shooting.

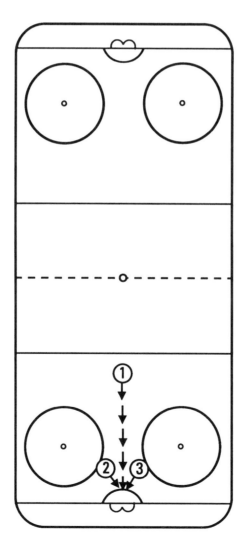

86. Simulated double rebound shooting

Player 1 passes to 2 who shoots on goal. After player 2's shot 3 shoots and then 4 shoots. 3 and 4 have a supply of pucks to keep the drill moving.

Coaching Notes: Good drill for goaltenders to practice playing the first shot and the rebounds. The extra pucks at 3 and 4 make certain the goaltender will have a rebound shot.

Variation: Players 3 and 4 play the tip-in before they shoot. This is an excellent goalie drill.

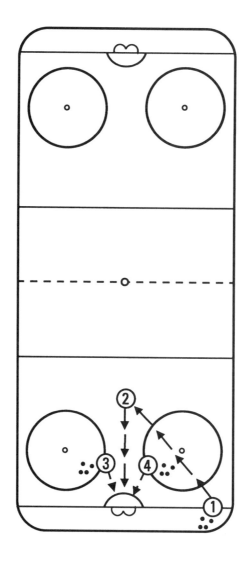

6
Individual Drills

87. Mirror drills

88. Stick checking

89. Pass the square-man in center

90. Puck chase and backchecking

91. Catch the attacker

92. Looping to backcheck drill

93. Backchecking from pass to wing

94. Sponge puck blocking shot drill

95. Defenseman pivot and chase

96. Puck retrieval drill for defensemen

97. Battle drill

98. Simple corner puck possession drill

99. Complex corner puck possession drill

100. Behind the net forechecking

101. Triangle keep away

102. 1-on-1 keep away

103. 3-on-3 keep away

104. 1-on-1

105. Partners 1-on-1 from side boards

106. 1-on-1 against pivoting defenseman

107. 2-on-0 with backchecker

108. 2-on-1 using half ice

109. 2-on-1 with backchecker

110. 2-on-1 from around the net

111. 2-on-2

112. 2-on-2 with backchecker

113. Puck throw at goalie

114. Close goalie passing

87. Mirror drills

Individual—Players 1 and 2 are partners. Either player may serve as the leader while the other mirrors every move he makes. The leader should make quick agility moves for difficulty and interest.

Team—Player A leads the team through various mirror maneuvers and skills. This can be done with or without a puck.

Coaching Notes: These are reaction or reflex drills. Unless the players respond as quickly as possible, the drill is useless.

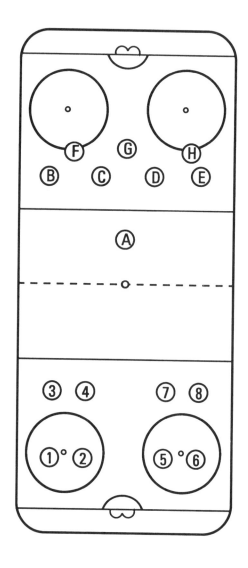

88. Stick checking

Stationary — Players work in pairs within a certain area.

Mobile — Player A attacks and 1 stick checks him. As they reach the end, they move to the boards, out of the way, and return to the end of the line.

Coaching Notes: This drill focuses on stickchecking. Since the players are stationary, skating is not a factor. This drill also helps in timing of the stickchecks while the puck carrier develops skill in avoiding the stickcheck.

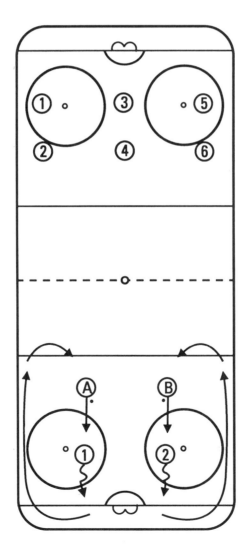

89. Pass the square — man in the center

The players pass the puck around while A tries to intercept the puck.

Coaching Notes: Although this is an excellent quick passing drill, the main emphasis is on the defensive skills of the man in the center. The passers must try to deceive the defender, and the defender must not commit himself until he can make a positive play.

Variation: No player in the center.

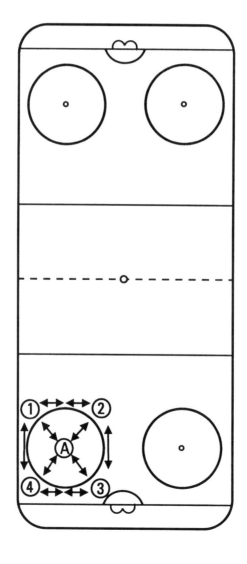

90. Puck chase and backchecking

The puck is pushed or placed ahead for 1 and 2 to break for. Whoever gets the puck becomes the shooter while the other becomes the backchecker.

Coaching Notes: This is a competitive drill and an excellent one-on-one situation. Fighting for the puck is basic to the game of ice hockey.

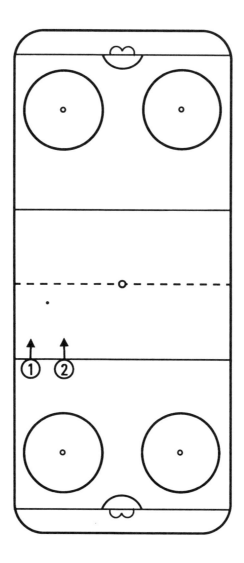

91. Catch the attacker

Player 1 attacks the goal. A tries to catch up and stop him.

Coaching Notes: This is a backchecking drill. Backchecking is not a fun part of the game, but it is an essential part of the game.

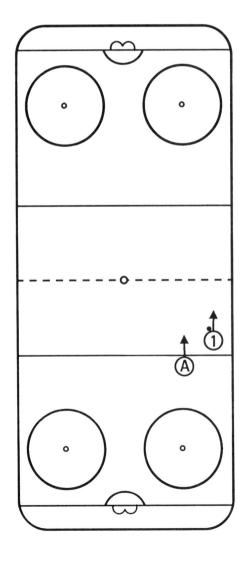

92. Looping to backcheck drill

Player 1 carries the puck out of the end zone. A loops in over the blue line and backchecks.

Coaching Notes: This is another backchecking drill that parallels a game situation where a player must change directions and pick up a check. Looping to pick up a check requires good timing and positional skating to achieve the proper angle of approach to the check.

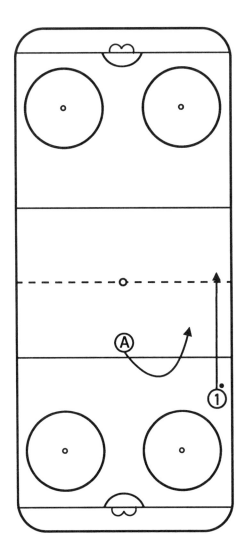

93. Backchecking from pass to wing

Player C passes to 1. A loops in and backchecks 1. C then moves to A's position while 2 moves to C's position.

Coaching Notes: Similar to drill number 92 except a passing play is involved. This is good for the pass receiver as he develops skill in receiving a pass while a backchecker is attacking him.

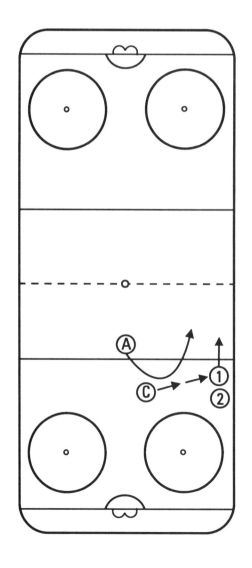

94. Sponge puck blocking shot drill

To practice blocking shots on goal it is safer to use sponge pucks. A blocks shots from 1, 2, and 3. Shots may come in sequence; however, it is best if the coach calls out the shooter's number. This is a good agility drill for A.

Coaching Notes: Using sponge pucks gives the players a chance to work on puck blocking technique without the fear of real pucks.

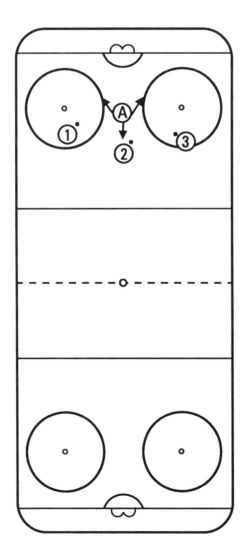

95. Defenseman pivot and chase.

Player 1 breaks along boards. A skates backwards and then pivots to check 1.

Coaching Notes: This drill is to focus on the defenseman stopping an attacker by backward skating, pivoting, and chasing or angling the puck carrier to nullify the attack. The key to this drill is usually the pivot. The pivot must be developed to a high efficiency.

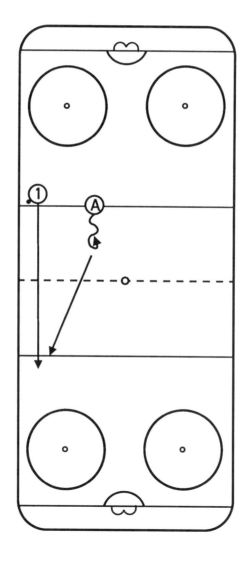

96. Puck retrieval drill for defensemen

Players 1 and 2 backward skate to about half way to the goal, pivot and break to the corner, stop and take puck to stickhandle it to the blue line. The puck is left on the blue line and the player repeats the drill. As soon as 1 and 2 are on their way, 3 and 4 can start. Players must also repeat from the other side.

Coaching Notes: This is a defenseman's situation drill. The skating backwards, pivoting, and skating forward to the corner is a common game occurrence. Speed is essential to gain puck control and a breakout play.

Variations:

1. Without the puck.
2. Have the defenseman 1 and 2 pass to a wing breaking along the boards to give a game situation drill.

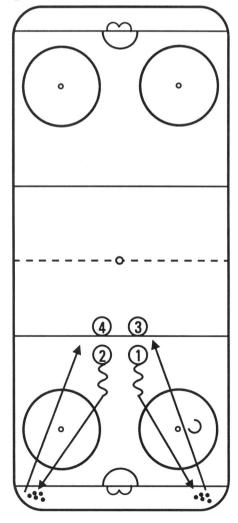

97. Battle drill

The puck is placed behind the defenseman A. Player 1 is a forward and must try to get to the puck to score on the goalie. A cannot hit the puck away, he must protect it from 1.

Coaching Notes: Excellent one-on-one drill to replicate a game scramble in front of the net.

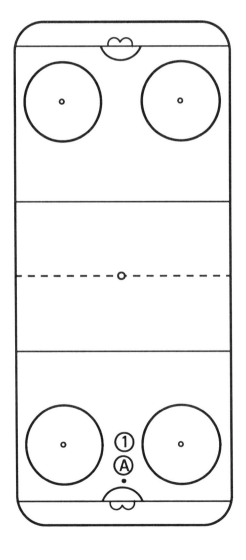

98. Simple corner puck possession drill

Player A and 1 go into the corner to gain puck possession. A can be a defenseman and 1 a forward. This drill can also be done with B and 2 very close together.

Coaching Notes: Control the corners and you can control the game. This is a one-on-one drill for practice in controlling the corners.

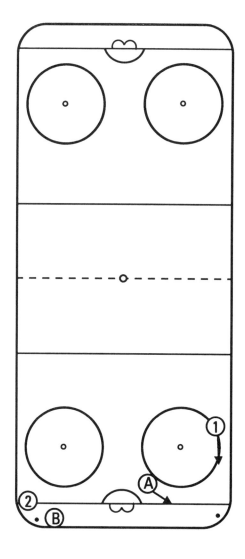

99. Complex corner puck possession drill

2-on-1 offensive—Game situations should be devised for this drill. A is a defenseman and 1 and 2 are attacking forwards trying to get the puck.

2-on-1 defensive—This can also be done with C as the backchecker working with B the defenseman. 3 is the attacker. Other game situation corner plays should be practiced.

Coaching Notes: This is a game situation corner practice. Usually it is best if the first forward plays the body of the defenseman while the other forward plays the puck.

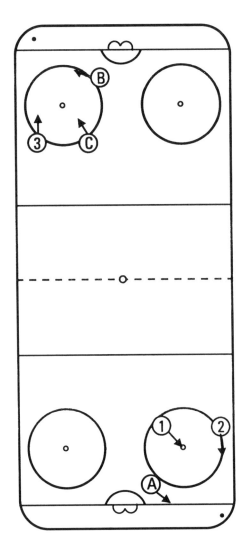

100. Behind the net forechecking

Player 1 carries the puck behind the goal net to breakout. A angles in on 1 and forechecks 1 as he breaks out.

Coaching Notes: With the puck behind the net so often, attackers must learn how to control the situation and prevent the puck from advancing up the ice. Timing is the key to this type of game situation.

Variations:

1. Player 1 cannot stop behind net.
2. Player 1 must stop and exit other side.
3. Player 1 must stop and exit either side.
4. Player 1 has any choice he desires.

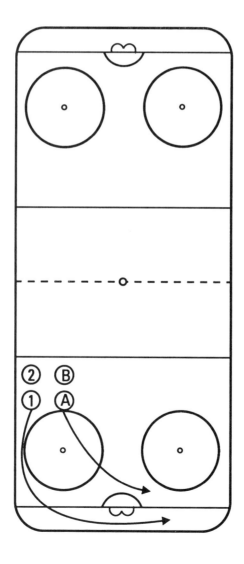

101. Triangle keep away

Players 1, 2, and 3 keep the puck away from player A who tries to intercept the puck.

A variation of the keep-away drills. It is a defensive drill.

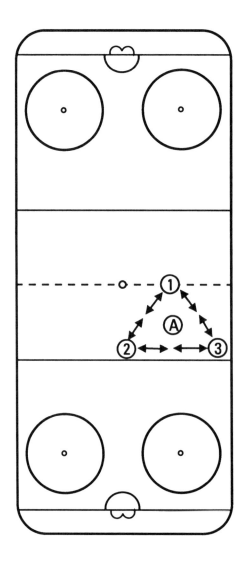

102. 1-on-1 keep away

This can be done with the use of sticks (stickhandling) or with the feet only. Keep away with the feet is good for developing balance and agility.

Coaching Notes: Do not let the player take big kicks at the puck when passing the puck with the feet. The big kick may hit another player.

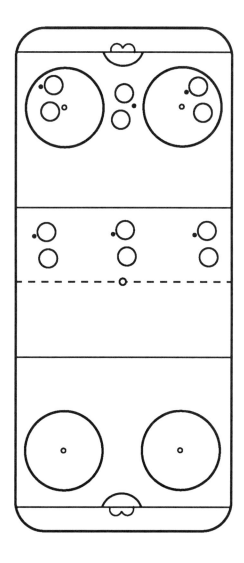

103. 3-on-3 keep away

Players 1, 2, and 3 keep the puck away from A, B, and C but must remain in their area (between the blue lines). Once A, B and C gain puck possession they attempt to keep it away from 1, 2, and 3.

Coaching Notes: This is a good passing and defensive practice drill. At a fast pace, it can be a conditioning drill.

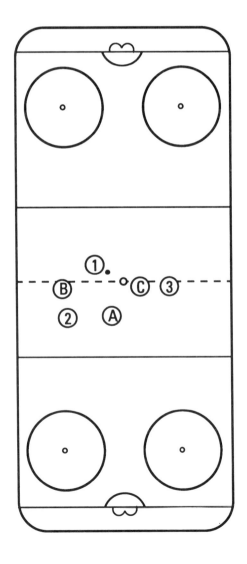

104. 1-on-1

From the corner — Players 1 and 4 attack while A and E defend. The next defensemen wait in the center of the ice out of the way.

Coaching Notes: This is a basic one-on-one drill. This drill is also a good warm-up drill.

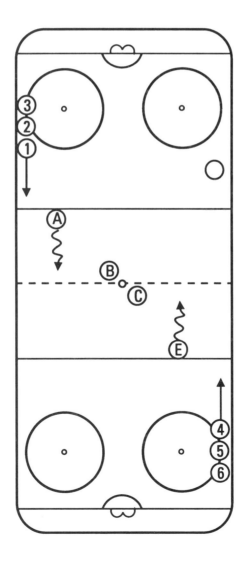

105. Partners 1-on-1 from side boards

Player A skates backwards and 1 skates forwards and tries to pass A. On reaching the other side, 1 skates backwards and A skates forwards. This drill can be used for contact or speed. It can be done with or without a puck.

Coaching Notes: This drill, when executed properly, is an excellent conditioning drill as all the players are active. With the use of pucks, the drill becomes a conditioning drill and a skill training drill.

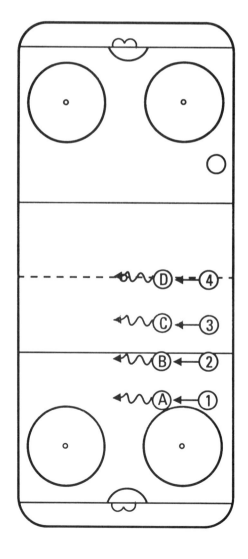

106. 1-on-1 against pivoting defenseman

Player 1 receives a pass from 2 and breaks for the goal. D breaks with forward skating and pivots to backward skating to play 1.

Coaching Notes: A game situation drill with the attacker receiving a pass to beat the defenseman while the defenseman tries to stop the attack. Again, timing is crucial to execution.

Variation: Player D uses a hockey stick with the blade cut off to force a body checking situation.

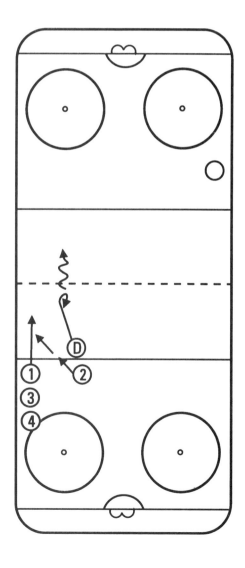

107. 2-on-0 with a backchecker

Players 1 and 2 attack the goal in a 2-on-0 situation. A is the backchecker and tries to prevent the attack on goal.

Coaching Notes: The focus is on backchecking. A rule by many teams is that the goaltender has the puck carrier while the backchecker has the other player.

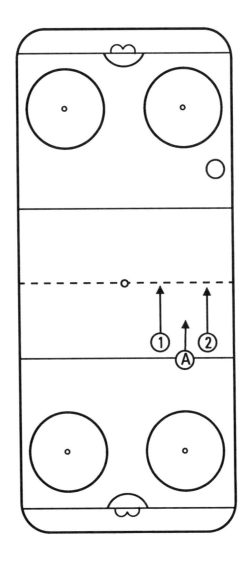

108. 2-on-1 using half ice

From corner — Players 1 and 2 break down the ice against 3.

From behind the net — Player A circles the net and uses the give and go with B for a 2-on-1 against C.

Coaching Notes: Basic two on one game situation. Emphasize position play. Do not let the attackers get too close, maintain triangulation with one deep and one close to the net. The defender must not get pulled to the boards and must backup on his line to the goalpost. Also the defender must not screen his goaltender.

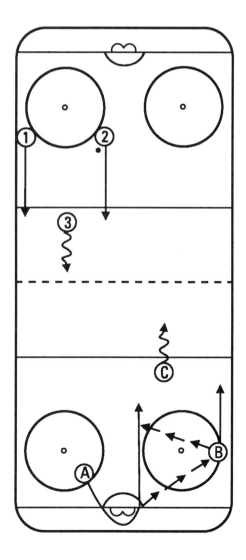

109. 2-on-1 with backchecker

From center — 1 and 2 advance against 4. 3 is the backchecker and he can start in between 1 and 2 or from the side of either one.

From behind the net — A circles behind the net and uses the give and go with B. D is the defenseman and C is the backchecker.

Coaching Notes: The rules of drill number 108 apply. Usually the backchecker plays the puck carrier while the defenseman covers the other attacker. The backchecker and defenseman must have a strategy to prevent confusion.

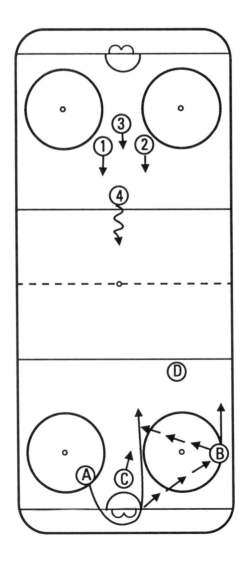

110. 2-on-1 from around the net

Players 1 and 2 are the attackers while A is the defender. 2 must carry the puck around the net to begin play on the near goal.

This is a good agility drill for defensemen.

Coaching Notes: Good drill for game situation scrambles around the goal.

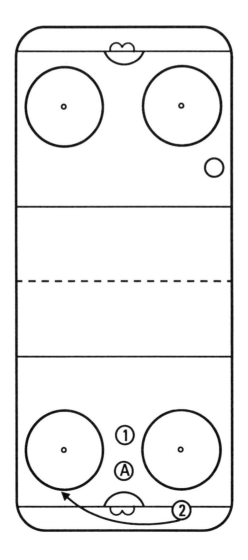

111. 2-on-2

From center—Players 1 and 2 advance against 5 and 6.

From behind the net—Player A circles the net and uses the give and go with B to begin the attack against D and C.

Coaching Notes: Two-on-two situations usually breakdown into two one-on-one situations.

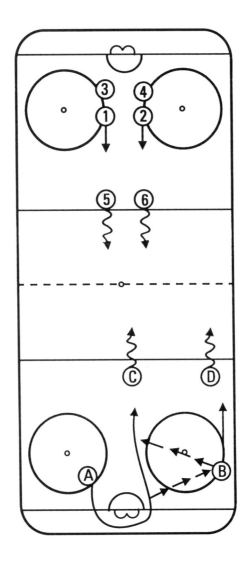

112. 2-on-2 with backchecker

From center—Players 1 and 2 attack. 3 and 4 are the defensemen while 5 is the backchecker.

From behind the net—Player A rounds in back of the net and uses the give and go with B. D and E are the defensemen and C is the backchecker.

Coaching Notes: More game situations of attacking with a backchecker and defending with a backchecker. Basic rules apply to prevent confusion of duties: defense each play a man while the backchecker plays the puck carrier.

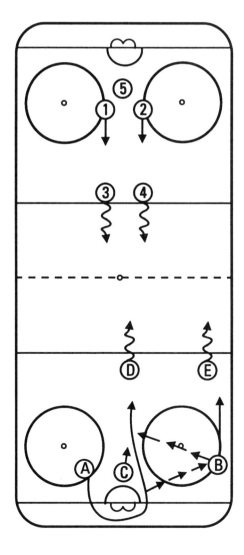

113. Puck throw at goalie

The coach or the other goalie throws pucks at various points of the goal. This is especially good when working on a particular move by the goalie when puck placement is important.

Coaching Notes: The pucks are thrown to give accuracy of puck placement.

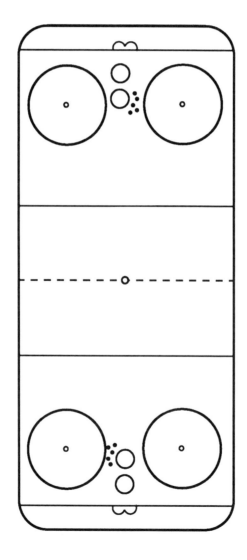

114. Close goalie passing

Players 1, 2, and 3 pass the puck around before shooting on goal. More than three passers can be used.

Coaching Notes: The goalie in reacting to the puck gets a good agility workout. It's also an excellent drill for goalie conditioning.

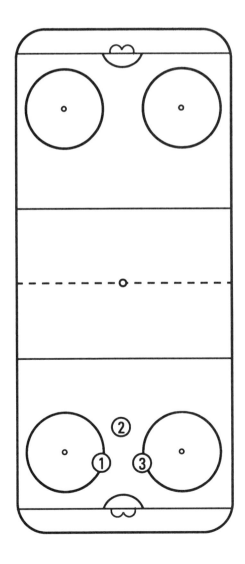

7

Team Drills

115. Face-off drills
116. 3-on-0 both ways
117. 3-on-0 half ice attacks
118. 3-on-0 with two pucks
119. 3-on-1 with late shooter
120. 3-on-2
121. 3-on-2 with backchecker
122. 3-on-2 from the slot shot
123. 3-on-2 close in play
124. 3-on-3 scrimmage
125. 3-on-4 backchecking drill
126. Team breakout 5-on-0
127. 5-on-0 single puck passing drill
128. 5-on-0 single puck passing drill with 3-on-2 return

129. 5-on-0 multiple puck passing drill
130. Team forecheck patterns
131. End zone play
132. Penalty killing
133. Power play drill
134. Pulled goalie drill
135. Sixth attacker drill
136. Body checking emphasis
137. Delayed penalty drill
138. Broken stick drill
139. Line change practice
140. Injury drill

115. Face-off drills

Individual—This is often best done with the blue line or the red line separating each contestant (e.g. 1 and 2). The winner of the draw is the player who controls the puck to his side of the line.

Face-off players should:

1. Pull puck to the right.

2. Pull puck to the left.

3. Push puck to the left.

4. Push puck to the right.

Team — Practice should be at all face-off points and also in pulled goalie situations.

Coaching Notes: Face-offs are extremely important in gaining puck possession. Do not neglect this phase of the game.

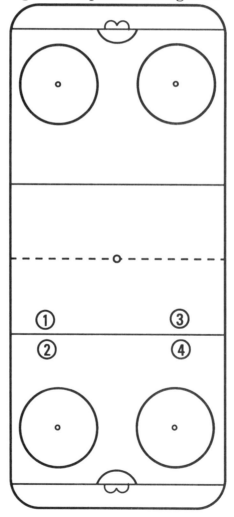

116. 3-on-0 both ways

Player F picks up the puck, rounds the net and breaks up the ice with A and C as wings. Once A, C, and F shoot at the far goalie, 5 picks up a puck and breaks up the ice with 1 and 3 as wings to attack the other goalie. The lines continue in this back and forth pattern.

Coaching Notes: Three-on-one drills are lead-up drills to the more complex game situation attacks. Use the three-on-one drills to develop position play patterns. Since there are no defenders, do not let the attackers be careless in their positioning and passing combinations.

Variations:

1. Players F, A, and B and 5, 1, and 3 can leave at the same time and pass against each other at mid-ice.

2. 3-on-1 and 3-on-2 can also be done to this pattern. The defensemen simply move out from the side boards.

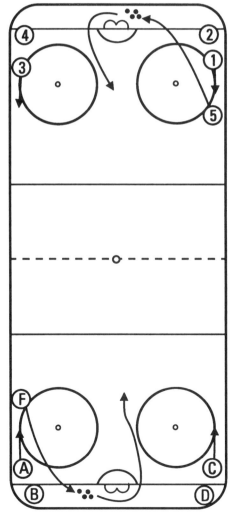

117. 3-on-0 half ice attacks

The lines attack from center ice to the goal.

Center plays slot—Player C passes to wing A and plays the slot. The far winger breaks for the goal.

Center breaks for the net—Player 1, after passing to 2, breaks for the net while the far winger 3 plays the slot.

The players can change lines to give practice in the other positions.

Coaching Notes: By using only half of the ice, the drill allows the players more action. The key to player movement is the centerman. If the centerman drifts for a two-on-one, the opposite winger breaks for the goal. If the centerman breaks for the goal, the far winger drifts to the slot. The far winder must monitor his centerman to determine his movement.

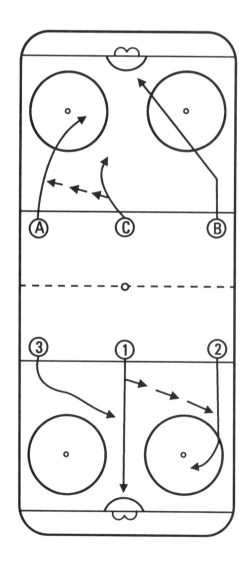

118. 3-on-0 with two pucks

Players 1, 2, and 3 advance up the ice for a 3-on-0 rush by passing two pucks to each other.

Coaching Notes: Two pucks force pressure on the situation. Two pucks also means that the players must be accurate or the drill breaks down.

Variations:

1. Various passing combinations can be used besides the one diagrammed. Such things as clockwise and counterclockwise passing patterns can be fun and beneficial.

2. This drill can be done with a 3-on-1 or a 3-on-2 attack.

3. Players 1, 2, and 3 advance up one side of the ice while three other players come down the other side.

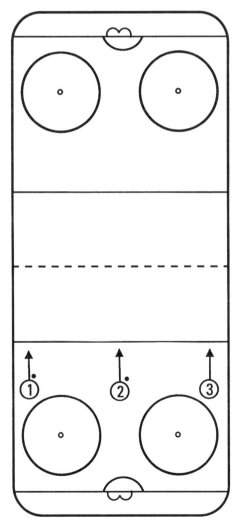

119. 3-on-1 with late shooter

Players 2, 3, and 4 rush against the defender A for a 3-on-1 attack. Player 1 comes up late and takes a shot on goal after the 3-on-1 has their attack and shot on goal. Players 2, 3, and 4 play tip-in or rebound from 1's shot.

Coaching Notes: The late shooter gives extra action to the goaltender and rebound practice to the attackers.

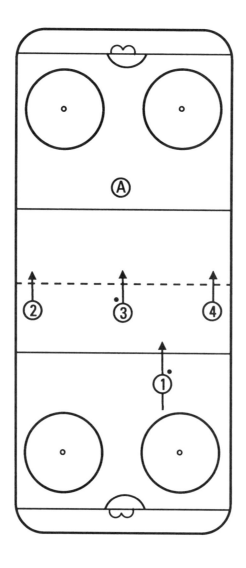

120. 3-on-2

Center with puck—Player 3 picks up the puck and carries it around the net for a 3-on-2 attack with 1 and 2 as wings. 4 and 5 are the defenders.

Pass from corner—Player A loops in to begin attack with B and C by receiving a pass from D in the corner. E and F are the defenders. This drill can be done both ways as explained under 3-on-0 Both Ways. This can also be done as a 3-on-1.

Coaching Notes: This is a basic game situation drill. If the drill is kept moving quickly it can be an excellent conditioning and training drill. Positional play is imperative. Do not let the players be careless in execution.

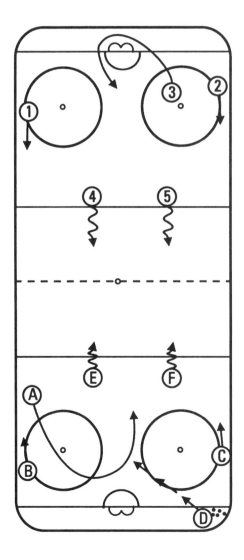

121. 3-on-2 with a backchecker

This is the same as the 3-on-2 drill except a backchecker 6, and player G is added to help the defensemen.

Coaching Notes: A game situation drill that focuses on positional play and timing. Coordination of the defensemen and the backchecker must be emphasized.

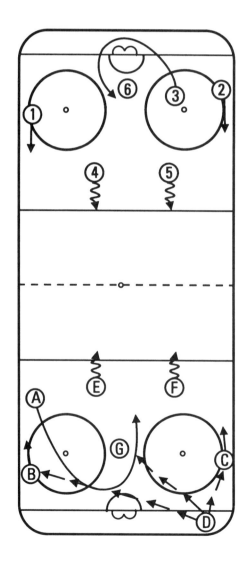

122. 3-on-2 from the slot shot

Player 1 shoots on goal with 2 and 3 playing the tip-in, screen, and rebound. A and B defend the goal area.

Coaching Notes: A game situation scramble drill. Excellent for goaltenders. Do not let A and B screen the goaltender.

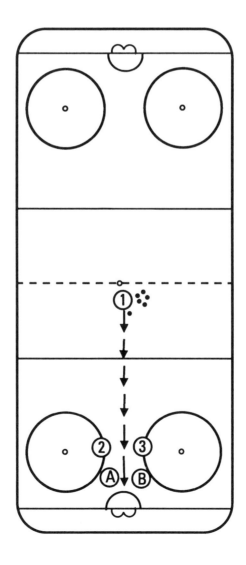

123. 3-on-2 close in play

Players 1, 2, and 3 try to score while A and B defend. This drill is very mobile and especially good for scramble play.

Coaching Notes: This is another scramble drill. Scramble drills are important as so much of the game is played in goalmouth scrambles.

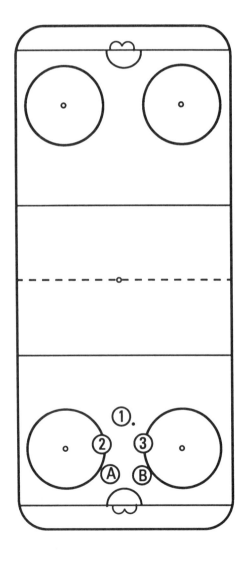

124. 3-on-3 scrimmage

Two teams of three players each scrimmage against each other. A time limit of 60 seconds or 90 seconds can be used as a player change to keep the players active. Develop quick changes to keep things moving.

Coaching Notes: This is an excellent conditioner as well as good activity for goalies. Very often this is a fun drill as the game is wide open.

Variation: Players change on the go, by a special whistle command, to prevent any stoppage of play.

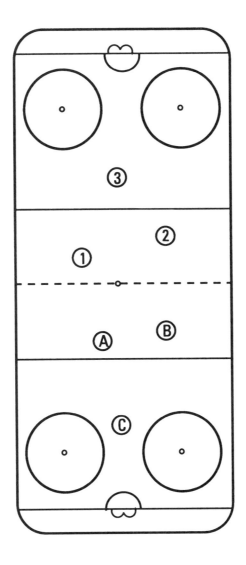

125. 3-on-4 backchecking drill

Players 1, 2, and 3 breakout for their attack on goal. C and D, the backcheckers, peel out for their duties while A and B play defense.

Coaching Notes: Emphasis is on backchecking. Positional play and timing must be worked on.

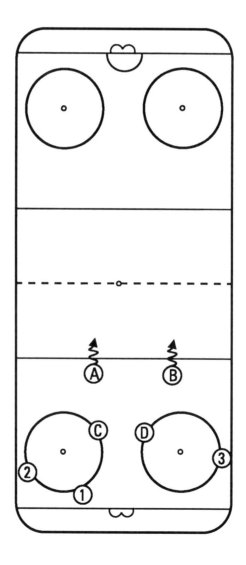

126. Team breakout 5-on-0

The puck is shot into the end zone for the team to breakout and attack the far goal.

Coaching Notes: These are breakout play drills that progress from no resistance to full resistance. Use the "5-on-0" to develop the pattern and then gradually add increasing resistance. Demand precise positional play for the various situations. With no resistance or only one of two defenders, it is easy to be careless in positional play and yet accomplish the attack. The little or no resistance is for development in the five-on-five situation.

Variations:

1. **5-on-1** — one player forechecks
2. **5-on-2** — two players forecheck
3. **5-on-3** — three players forecheck
4. **5-on-4** — four players forecheck
5. **5-on-5** — five players forecheck

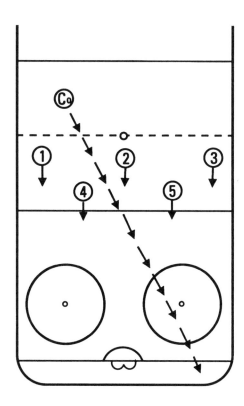

127. 5-on-0 single puck passing drill

Five players attack the goal with set requirements, e.g. six passes, and each player must touch the puck once; or ten passes and each player must touch the puck twice.

Coaching Notes: The requirements are to pressure the players into quick, accurate passes.

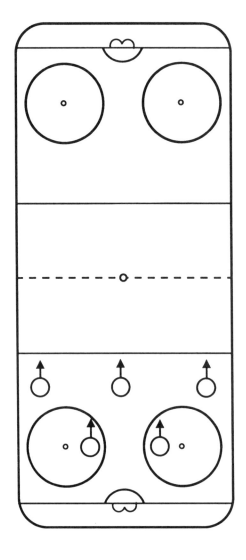

128. 5-on-0 single puck passing drill with 3-on-2 return

The players do the 5-on-0 single passing drill up the ice. After their attack on the goal the forwards 1, 2, and 3 regroup for their return of a 3-on-2 against the two defensemen 4 and 5.

Coaching Notes: Excellent player movement drill and conditioner.

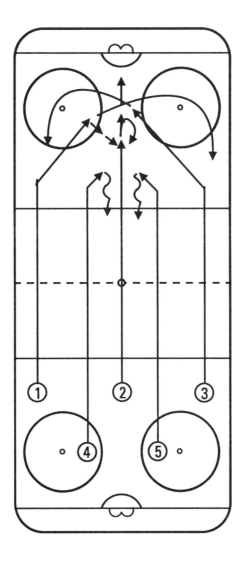

129. 5-on-0 multiple puck passing drill

This passing drill is a 5-on-0 rush up the ice with continuous passing. Gradually two pucks are used, then three, etc. If desired, another unit can come down the ice from the opposite direction.

Coaching Notes: This is a fun drill, but it also develops quickness and accuracy in passing.

Variation: Use a 4-on-0 attack with units coming in both directions.

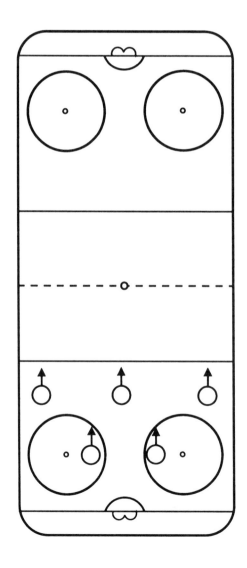

130. Team forecheck patterns

- **3-on-2**—Players 1, 2, and 3 move into forecheck pattern as D1 and D2 try to breakout.
- **5-on-3**—Five players forecheck three players breaking out.
- **5-on-4**—Five players forecheck four players trying to breakout.
- **5-on-5**—Five players forecheck five players trying to breakout.

Coaching Notes: The emphasis is on forechecking. Precision of movement is important whether there are two, three, four, or five players breaking out.

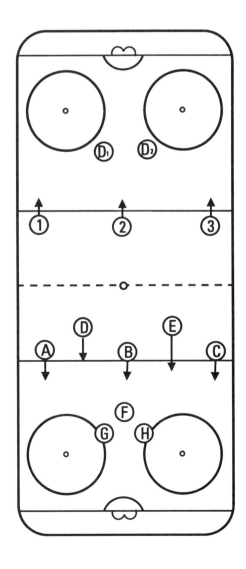

131. End zone play

Game strategy can be practiced at each end of the ice in the end zones.

Coaching Notes: Using both ends gets more player action. Positional play is imperative.

132. Penalty killing

In many cases this can be done with the power play drills. Both one man short and two men short must be practiced.

Coaching Notes: The game situation is the drill.

133. Power play drill

Power play patterns are best if the opposition is gradually increased. Start off with 5-on-0 to establish the pattern or idea. Then increase the opposition to a 5-on-1 situation, then a 5-on-2, and a 5-on-3, with the 5-on-4 as the actual game pattern. The power play in a pulled goalie situation should also be practiced.

Coaching Notes: The trend in the power play is to move quickly but not to rush the play. Timing of movement and passes may well be the key to power play efficiency.

134. Pulled goalie drill

Any game situation involving a pulled goalie should be practiced. This involves offensive and defensive play. Practice with the goalie quickly leaving the net for the sixth attacker coming over the boards is essential. Face-off positioning and practice is very important.

Coaching Notes: Although the pulled goalie situation is not too common, it must be practiced for when the occasion does arise. Too many coaches and players assume because they have the extra attacker, they have an advantage. This is not true. Teams must practice in how to effectively use the extra attacker.

135. Sixth attacker drill

Various team drills, end zone play and scrimmage can be utilized to practice the sixth attacker change with the goalie. An arm signal by the coach or a time limit (e.g. ten seconds) or a command (as soon as the puck is over the red line, change) can be used as a signal for the change.

Coaching Notes: The transition during play of the goaltender coming out and a sixth attacker coming over the boards must be practiced. Never assume that this transition will be efficient during game conditions. Practice for efficiency.

136. Body checking emphasis

To emphasize playing the man or bodychecking, have the bodycheckers use sticks with the blades cut off. This forces them to play the man.

Coaching Notes: Players with the blades cut of their hockey sticks must body check with the stick down and safely positioned. This drill is excellent in teaching body play.

137. Delayed penalty drill

This is a game situation and should be practiced. Often a pulled goalie situation will take place.

Coaching Notes: Goals have been scored by pulling the goalie for an extra attacker when the opposition has a delayed penalty. Panic must not prevail during a game so practice this situation during training. Efficiency, timing, and precision are imperative.

138. Broken stick drill

Practice the broken stick situation especially in the defensive end zone. Have a player drop his stick or take his stick away while scrimmage progresses.

Coaching Notes: If it can happen during a game then it must be practiced.

139. Line change practice

Scrimmage, team drills or end zone play can practice the line change. The line change can be signaled by a whistle (a different sound than the regular whistle) or by a command at the face-off (e.g. line change in fifteen seconds).

Coaching Notes: Line changes on the go are extremely important. Inefficient and slow line changes are detrimental to team play.

140. Injury drill

Occasionally practice should be provided in getting a whistle or stoppage in play in the event a player is injured or unable to participate in the action.

MASTERS PRESS

DEAR VALUED CUSTOMER,

Masters Press is dedicated to bringing you timely and authoritative books for your personal and professional library. As a leading publisher of sports and fitness books, our goal is to provide you with easily accessible information on topics that interest you written by the most qualified authors. You can assist us in this endeavor by checking the box next to your particular areas of interest.

We appreciate your comments and will use the information to provide you with an expanded and more comprehensive selection of titles.

Thank you very much for taking the time to provide us with this helpful information.

Cordially,
Masters Press

Areas of interest in which you'd like to see Masters Press publish books:

☐ COACHING BOOKS
 Which sports? What level of competition?

☐ INSTRUCTIONAL/DRILL BOOKS
 Which sports? What level of competition?

☐ FITNESS/EXERCISE BOOKS
 ☐ Strength—Weight Training
 ☐ Body Building
 ☐ Other

☐ REFERENCE BOOKS
 what kinds?

☐ BOOKS ON OTHER
 Games, Hobbies
 or Activities

Are you more likely to read a book or watch a video-tape to get the sports information you are looking for?

I'm interested in the following sports as a participant:

I'm interested in the following sports as an observer:

Please feel free to offer any comments or suggestions to help us shape our publishing plan for the future.

Name _____ Age _____

Address _____

City _____ State _____ Zip _____

Daytime phone number _____

BUSINESS REPLY MAIL

FIRST CLASS MAIL   PERMIT NO. 1317   INDIANAPOLIS IN

POSTAGE WILL BE PAID BY ADDRESSEE

MASTERS PRESS

2647 WATERFRONT PKY EAST DR

INDIANAPOLIS IN 46209-1418

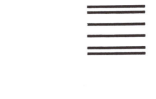

NO POSTAGE
NECESSARY
IF MAILED
IN THE
UNITED STATES